Congressional
Research
Service

U.S. Trade Remedy Laws and Nonmarket Economies: A Legal Overview

Jeanne J. Grimmett
Legislative Attorney

May 23, 2012

Congressional Research Service
7-5700
www.crs.gov
RL33976

CRS Report for Congress
Prepared for Members and Committees of Congress

Summary

Two major U.S. trade remedies are antidumping (AD) law, which combats the sale of imported products at less than their fair market value, and countervailing duty (CVD) law, which aims to offset foreign government subsidization of imported goods. If dumped or subsidized imports are found to cause or threaten material injury to a domestic industry, antidumping or countervailing duties will be imposed. Both remedies are available when goods are imported from competitor countries with free market policies. As of 1984, however, only AD law had been applied to goods from nonmarket or "transitional" economies (NMEs). With the continued economic growth of some of these economies, such as China and Vietnam, pressure increased on the U.S. government to use both trade remedies more aggressively against unfair imports from these countries.

AD law has been amended several times since its inception in 1921. With Congress's continued statutory guidance, the Department of Commerce (DOC) has implemented several different methodologies for applying AD law, including using surrogate country data when the fair market value of a product in the originating country is not readily ascertainable. CVD law had not been used against NMEs, however, since DOC concluded in 1984 that it could not determine subsidization in such situations. In 1986, the U.S. Court of Appeals for the Federal Circuit (CAFC), in *Georgetown Steel Corp. v. United States*, upheld DOC's interpretation of the CVD statute as reasonable. While DOC had generally refused to review CVD petitions against NME countries following this determination, it accepted a petition seeking a CVD on imports of coated free-sheet paper from China in 2006. DOC distinguished the current Chinese economy from the Soviet-style economies at issue in *Georgetown Steel* and found that the imported Chinese paper was subsidized. Although the U.S. International Trade Commission did not make the requisite final affirmative material injury determination in this case, subsequent CVD petitions were successful, resulting in the imposition of 24 CVD orders on NME merchandise.

World Trade Organization (WTO) agreements, together with the WTO Accession Protocols of China and Vietnam, acknowledge that AD and CV duties may be imposed on these countries' goods, and that surrogate country data may be used to calculate dumping margins or subsidization. In a WTO case brought by China, however, the WTO Appellate Body found in an April 2011 report that the simultaneous imposition by the United States of AD and CV duties on the same Chinese merchandise, where surrogate country data was used to establish the fair market value of the goods in the AD case, remedied the same subsidization twice or "double counted" in violation of U.S. WTO obligations. More broadly, the CAFC held in December 2011 that CVDs may not be imposed on NME goods under any circumstance, finding in *GPX Int'l Tire Corp. v. United States* that Congress had legislatively ratified DOC's 1984 statutory interpretation and thus DOC could not interpret the statute to permit such duties. The CAFC affirmed a lower court decision that also prohibited DOC from imposing CVDs on NME goods, but did so because DOC had not eliminated double counting, the practice at issue in the WTO dispute. The Administration asked Congress to enact remedial legislation and, on March 5, 2012, requested that the CAFC rehear the *GPX* case. Congress responded quickly, enacting P.L. 112-99, signed March 13, 2012, which generally authorizes CVDs for NME goods, makes this authority effective as of November 20, 2006, and prospectively amends AD law to address double counting issues. DOC is preparing WTO-compliant determinations in China's WTO case and has stated that implementation of the new law will be a factor in this compliance effort. The United States did not fully comply by the April 25 deadline in the case, however, and has agreed to facilitate any WTO compliance review requested by China. On May 9, 2012, the CAFC remanded the *GPX* case to the lower court to address constitutional issues stemming from the different effective dates in the new law.

Contents

Introduction

Two major U.S. trade remedies, each set out in Title VII of the Tariff Act of 1930, are antidumping (AD) law, which combats the sale of imported goods at less than their fair market value, and countervailing duty (CVD) law, which is aimed at offsetting foreign government subsidization of imported items. If dumped or subsidized imports are found to cause material injury, or threat, to a domestic industry, and the dumping margin or the net subsidy is not *de minimis*, antidumping or countervailing duties will be imposed.[1] Both remedies are available when goods are imported from competitor countries that have free market policies. Since 1984, however, only AD law had been applied to goods from nonmarket or other "transitional" economies. With the continued economic growth of some of these economies, such as China and Vietnam, pressure has increased on the U.S. government to utilize both domestic trade remedies more aggressively against unfair imports from these countries.

This report (1) discusses the application of antidumping and countervailing duty law to the goods of nonmarket economy (NME) countries, including the decision of the Department of Commerce (DOC) in 2007 to change its long-standing policy and apply CVD law to such goods; (2) reviews China's successful case in the World Trade Organization challenging the U.S. application of CVDs to Chinese products and the status of U.S. compliance efforts in the case; (3) examines the December 2011 decision of the U.S. Court of Appeals for the Federal Circuit in *GPX Int'l Tire Corp. v. United States* holding that the U.S. CVD law does not authorize DOC to apply CVDs to NME country goods; (4) summarizes the subsequently enacted P.L. 112-99, signed March 13, 2012, a statute authorizing DOC to apply CVDs to such products; and (5) notes recent developments in the *GPX* litigation.

Antidumping (AD) Law and Nonmarket Economies

Background

As generally applied, antidumping (AD) law considers dumping to have occurred when a foreign manufacturer charges a price for its product that is "less than its fair value" (LTFV).[2] For dumping that is alleged from market-based economies, DOC employs a standard methodology for determining a product's fair value. First, DOC determines whether a foreign manufacturer's goods were sold in the United States for LTFV by comparing the U.S. price of the product with "normal value,"[3] which is generally the price of the merchandise in the firm's domestic market.[4] If the product is not sold or offered for sale in the foreign firm's domestic market, DOC identifies the price at which the product is sold or offered for sale in countries other than the United States.[5]

---

[1] 19 U.S.C. §§1671, 1673 (2006). The general de minimis rate for subsidies is less than 1 percent, 19 U.S.C. §§1671d(a)(3), 1671b(b)(4)(A) (2006); for dumping margins, less than 2 percent, 19 U.S.C. §§1673d(a)(4), 1673b(b)(3)(2006).

[2] *See* 19 U.S.C. §1673 (2006).

[3] *See* 19 U.S.C. §1677b(a) (2006).

[4] *See* 19 U.S.C. §1677b(a)(1)(B)(i) (2006).

[5] *See* 19 U.S.C. §1677b(a)(1)(B)(ii) (2006).

Finally, if there are no sales in the home market or to third countries, the statute authorizes DOC to utilize a "constructed value."[6]

If DOC finds that dumping has occurred, it establishes the "dumping margin" by calculating the average amount by which the product's fair market value exceeds the price of the product in the United States.[7] The finding of dumping and the fixing of the "dumping margin" establish the first of the two prongs required to impose an AD duty. The final step in imposing an AD duty is an affirmative determination that the dumped imports have caused or threaten to cause material injury to a U.S. industry, or materially retard the establishment of an industry in the United States.[8] The injury determination is made by the U.S. International Trade Commission (ITC), an independent agency.

Application of AD Law to Nonmarket Economies: Various Approaches

As applied to nonmarket economies (NMEs), the standard methodology described above causes problems because nonmarket economies do not allocate resources according to traditional market concepts of supply and demand, thereby making determinations of fair market value almost impossible. From the adoption of the Antidumping Act of 1921[9] until the passage of the Trade Act of 1974,[10] the application of AD law to nonmarket economies was devised and implemented exclusively through administrative agency action, as the statutes were silent on the matter. In the 1960s, the Treasury Department, which at the time was the agency with responsibility over domestic trade remedy laws, developed and began using what was known as the "surrogate country" approach for applying AD law to NME countries. Under this approach, comparable prices and costs from similarly situated third countries were substituted for the NME country to determine fair market value.[11] This approach was adopted and codified by Congress in the Trade Act of 1974.[12] According to at least one legal scholar, "the surrogate methodology proved difficult to apply because there were occasions when there was no available surrogate. Therefore, it was necessary to devise an alternative methodology to use when an appropriate surrogate could not be located."[13]

The Treasury Department responded to the concerns raised by the "surrogate country" approach by adopting a new methodology in 1975. This methodology, known as the "factors of production" approach, required that the amount of each factor input be taken from a market economy country

---

[6] *See* 19 U.S.C. §1677b(a)(4) (2006) (defining the use of constructed value); 19 U.S.C. §1677b(e) (2006) (providing the method of calculating a constructed value).

[7] 19 U.S.C. §1677(35) (2006).

[8] *See* 19 U.S.C. §1677(7)(A) (2006) (stating that "[t]he term 'material injury' means harm which is not inconsequential, immaterial, or unimportant"). The statute requires that for threatened injuries the ITC may not base its determination on "mere conjecture or supposition." *See* 19 U.S.C. §1677(7)(F)(ii) (2006).

[9] Antidumping Act of 1921, ch. 14 §205, 42 Stat. 9, 13 (1921).

[10] Trade Act of 1974, P.L. 93-618, §321, 88 Stat. 1978, 2074 (1974).

[11] *See* Bicycles From Czechoslovakia, 25 *Federal Register* 6,657 (1960).

[12] *See* Trade Act of 1974, *supra* note 10.

[13] Robert H. Lantz, *The Search for Consistency Treatment of Nonmarket Economies in Transition under United States Antidumping and Countervailing Duty Laws*, 10 AM. U. J. INT'L L. & POL'Y 993, 1003 (1995).

---

considered to be at a comparable stage of economic development.[14] Congress expressly adopted this approach in the Trade Agreements Act of 1979, as an alternative to be used in NME cases where there was no available surrogate country.[15]

In 1988, Congress again acted to adopt new AD provisions for dealing with nonmarket economies. In the Omnibus Trade and Competitiveness Act of 1988 (OTCA),[16] Congress enacted numerous reforms to the antidumping laws, starting with a definition of a nonmarket economy country, as well as a set of standards that DOC was to take into consideration when determining whether a specific country qualified as such. According to the OTCA, a "nonmarket economy country" is a country that DOC determines "does not operate on market principles of cost or pricing structures, so that sales of merchandise in such country do not reflect the fair value of the merchandise."[17] The factors DOC must take into consideration when making a determination regarding a country's status as a nonmarket economy include

> (i) the extent to which the currency of the foreign country is convertible into the currency of other countries; (ii) the extent to which wage rates in the foreign country are determined by free bargaining between labor and management; (iii) the extent to which joint ventures or other investments by firms of other foreign countries are permitted in the foreign country; (iv) the extent of government ownership or control of the means of production; (v) the extent of government control over the allocation of resources and over the price and output decisions of enterprises; and (vi) such other factors as the administering authority [i.e., DOC] considers appropriate.[18]

In addition, the OTCA provides DOC with significant administrative discretion for determining when a foreign country is a nonmarket economy. According to the statute, the determination of NME status may be made "with respect to any foreign country at any time," and remains effective until expressly revoked by DOC.[19] Moreover, DOC's determinations are not subject to judicial review in any antidumping investigation.[20]

With respect to AD methodologies, the OTCA amended the AD laws to require that the "factors of production" approach was the preferred method of applying the law to nonmarket economies.[21]

---

[14] *See* Electric Golf Cars From Poland, 40 *Federal Register* 25,497 (1975).

[15] Trade Agreements Act of 1979, P.L. 96-39, §776, 93 Stat. 144, 186 (1979) (codified as amended at 19 U.S.C. §1677e). The act also transferred administrative authority from Treasury to the Department of Commerce (DOC), which issued regulations outlining the hierarchy of methodologies to be used in determining the fair market value in AD investigations involving nonmarket economies. According to DOC, market value should be determined according to (1) the home market prices of such or similar merchandise in a surrogate country; (2) the export price of such or similar merchandise shipped from a surrogate; (3) when actual or accurate prices are not available, the constructed value of such or similar merchandise in a surrogate country; and (4) the value in a surrogate country of the factors of production used in the nonmarket economy for such or similar merchandise. *See* 19 C.F.R. §353.8 (a)-(c) (1979).

[16] Omnibus Trade and Competitiveness Act of 1988, P.L. 100-418, 102 Stat. 1107 (1988).

[17] 19 U.S.C. §1677(18)(A) (2006).

[18] 19 U.S.C. §1677(18)(B) (2006).

[19] 19 U.S.C. §1677(18)(C) (2006).

[20] 19 U.S.C. §1677(18)(D) (2006).

[21] *See* 19 U.S.C. §1677b(c)(2006) (stating that when "(A) the subject merchandise is exported from a nonmarket economy country, and (B) the administering authority finds that available information does not permit the normal value of the subject merchandise to be determined ... the administering authority shall determine the normal value of the subject merchandise on the basis of the value of the factors of production utilized in producing the merchandise and to which shall be added an amount for general expenses and profit plus the cost of containers, coverings, and other expenses.").

Despite this express statutory change, however, DOC appears to have retained a significant amount of discretion with respect to its application. The legislative history of the OTCA seems to support DOC's broad claims of discretion, indicating that DOC is to determine on a case-by-case basis whether the available information permits the use of the standard methodology or whether a different approach is warranted.[22] As further evidence of its discretion to determine which approach to use when determining fair market value, DOC stated at the time that it would seek to value factors in the following order of priority:

> (1) prices paid by the NME manufacturer for items imported from a market economy; (2) prices in the primary surrogate country of domestically produced or imported materials; (3) prices in one or more secondary surrogate countries reported by the industry producing the subject merchandise in the secondary country or countries; and (4) prices in one or more secondary surrogate countries from sources other than the industry producing the subject merchandise.[23]

The adoption by Congress of a specific statute authorizing DOC to apply AD law to nonmarket economies, as well as the provision of legislative guidance with respect to acceptable methodologies—namely, authorizing various surrogate country approaches—had made AD law the exclusive remedy for U.S. industries when confronting unfair trade practices from nonmarket economies. As discussed below, however, the recent application—after a 23-year abstention by DOC—of countervailing duty law to China, a nonmarket economy, potentially provided adversely affected industries with another option for combating unfair trade practices from NME countries.

Countervailing Duty (CVD) Law and Nonmarket Economies (NMEs)

Background

Countervailing duty (CVD) laws are designed and intended to provide relief to domestic industries that have been materially injured, or are threatened with material injury, by imported goods that have been subsidized by a foreign government or other public entity. Specifically, the relief provided takes the form of an additional import duty on the subsidized imports. The duty levied is to be equal to the estimated amount of the government or other public subsidization. Similar to AD law, for an industry to obtain relief, both the ITC and DOC must make conclusive determinations.[24] DOC must find that the targeted imports have been subsidized, and ITC must find that the subsidized imports have caused material injury, or the threat of material injury, to a

---

[22] *See* S. Rep. No. 100-71, 100th Cong., 1st Sess., 108 (1987) (stating that the bill "does not prohibit the [DOC] from using its normal methodology for determining foreign market value in cases regarding nonmarket economy countries. If information submitted by a nonmarket economy country to the [DOC] permits foreign market value to be determined accurately using the normal methodology, then the Committee expects such methodology to be used by the [DOC]."); *see also* Conf. Report No. 100-576, 100th Cong., 2d Sess. 591 (1988).

[23] Final Determination of Sales at Less Than Fair Value: Sparklers from the People's Republic of China, 56 *Federal Register* 20,588, 20,590 (May 6, 1991). The department stated that "this ranking of data sources reflects the Department's desire to use to the greatest extent possible factor prices in a single surrogate country," but that that it was unable to do so for all inputs in the instant case. *Id.* at 20,590; *see also* 19 C.F.R. §351.408 (c)(2)(2011).

[24] 19 U.S.C. §1671 (2006).

domestic industry or have materially retarded the establishment of an industry in the United States.

Application of CVD Law to Nonmarket Economies

Unlike the AD laws, U.S. CVD laws had not been traditionally applied to nonmarket economies. This is largely as a result of a 1984 determination by DOC that there was no adequate way to measure market distortions caused by subsidies in an economy that is not based on market principles. The first determination by DOC regarding the application of CVD law to nonmarket economies involved carbon steel wire rods manufactured in Czechoslovakia and Poland, both of which were nonmarket economies at the time.[25] At the time of DOC's decision, the United States had two separate CVD statutes. The first, Section 303 of the Tariff Act of 1930,[26] applied

> ... [w]henever any country, dependency, colony, province, or other political subdivision of government, person, partnership, association, cartel, or corporation, shall pay or bestow, directly or indirectly, any bounty or grant upon the manufacture or production or export of any article or merchandise manufactured or produced in such country, dependency, colony, province, or other political subdivision of government.[27]

Section 303, which was applicable except in cases of merchandise imported from countries "under the Agreement" (see below), did not generally require a showing that the subsidized imports caused injury to a domestic industry.[28]

The second CVD statute, Section 701 of the Tariff Act of 1930, was enacted as part of the Trade Agreements Act of 1979 and was intended to bring the United States into compliance with the Agreement on the Interpretation and Application of Articles VI, XVI, and XXIII of the General Agreements on Tariffs and Trade (Subsidies Code), an agreement that had been negotiated in the 1970s during the Tokyo Round of Multilateral Trade Negotiations conducted under the auspices of the General Agreements on Tariffs and Trade (GATT).[29] Section 701(b) applied CVD law to "a country under the Agreement," meaning a country that was party to the Subsidies Code or other related agreements with the United States, and required that the United States also make a determination that the subsidized imports either caused, or threatened to cause, material injury to an industry in the United States, or materially retarded the establishment of an industry in the United States.[30]

---

[25] As many commentators have noted, however, this was not the first petition to be filed at DOC relating to a nonmarket economy. In 1983, there was a CVD petition involving textiles from China, which was withdrawn prior to a ruling by DOC. *See, e.g.,* Sanghan Wang, *U.S. Trade Laws Concerning Nonmarket Economies Revisited for Fairness and Consistency*, 10 EMORY INT'L L. REV. 593, 598 n. 27 (citing Judith Hippler Bello & Alan F. Holmer, THE ANTIDUMPING AND COUNTERVAILING DUTY LAWS: KEY LEGAL AND POLICY ISSUES 146-48 (1987)). For additional discussion of administrative action in CVD cases involving NME countries, see also CRS Report RL33550, *Trade Remedy Legislation Applying Countervailing Action to Nonmarket Economy Countries*, by Vivian C. Jones.

[26] *See* Tariff Act of 1930, ch. 479, §303 (1930). Section 303 of the Tariff Act of 1930 was repealed when the United States enacted the Uruguay Round Agreements Act of 1994 and subsequently joined the World Trade Organization. *See* Uruguay Round Agreements Act, P.L. 103-465, §261(a), 108 Stat. 4809 (1994).

[27] *See* Tariff Act of 1930, ch. 479, §303(a), as amended, 19 U.S.C. §1303(a) (1982).

[28] See Tariff Act of 1930, §303(a)-(b), as amended, 19 U.S.C. §1303(a)-(b) (1982).

[29] *See* Trade Agreements Act of 1979, P.L. 96-39, §§101, 103, 105(a), 93 Stat. 190, 193 (1979).

[30] *Id.*

Because neither Poland nor Czechoslovakia were signatories to the 1979 Subsidies Code, or fulfilled other related statutory criteria, DOC conducted its investigations of the alleged subsidization of carbon wire steel rod pursuant to Section 303 of the Tariff Act.[31] At the preliminary determination stage, DOC found that the phrase "any country" meant that no government entity could be excluded on a *per se* basis from the CVD law.[32] At the final determination stage, however, DOC indicated that it had failed to address a second jurisdictional element, namely, "whether government activities in a [nonmarket economy] confer a 'bounty or grant' within the meaning of section 303."[33] In evaluating this element, DOC determined that countervailable subsidies cannot, conceptually speaking, be found within a nonmarket economy and, therefore, cannot be included within the scope of the phrase "bounty or grant."[34]

To justify its final determinations, DOC relied on the rationale that a subsidy is an action taken by a government or other public entity that distorts or subverts the operation of the free market. Since all costs, prices, and profits in nonmarket economies are centrally controlled (i.e., by the state), the concept of subsidization is arguably meaningless as there are no market forces to subvert or distort. In other words, because a subsidy is essentially a market phenomena, it has no meaning or purpose in a nonmarket economy.[35] In addition, DOC maintained that, while resources may in fact be allocated inefficiently relative to a similarly developed market economy, it is impossible to state with any degree of certainty whether the misallocation results from subsidization, or from central planning.[36] DOC stated that because all economic activity in a nonmarket economy is centrally controlled, there exists no way practically to "disaggregate government action in such a way as to identify the exceptional action that is a subsidy."[37]

DOC, in determining that its conclusion was consistent with its statutory authority, conducted a review of the applicable CVD statutes and their legislative histories. Based on this review, DOC concluded that "Congress has never confronted directly the question of whether the countervailing duty law applies to [nonmarket economy] countries."[38] DOC pointed to amendments to U.S. trade remedy law made by Congress in both 1974 and 1979 to justify its determination. DOC noted in particular that, while Congress addressed trade disruption caused by surges of imports from NME countries by adopting Section 406 of the Trade Act of 1974 and addressed unfair competition from NME imports by making changes to the antidumping laws, it declined to make corresponding changes to CVD law.[39] Therefore, in light of Congress's silence with respect to the application of CVDs to imports from nonmarket economies, DOC concluded that, as the administering agency, it possessed broad discretionary authority with respect to the question of whether a countervailable subsidy could exist in a nonmarket economy situation.[40]

---

[31] Carbon Steel Wire Rod From Czechoslovakia; Final Negative Countervailing Duty Determination, 49 *Federal Register* 19,370, 19,371 (May 7, 1984).

[32] *Id.*

[33] *Id.*

[34] *Id.*

[35] *See id.*

[36] *Id.*

[37] *Id.* at 19,372.

[38] *Id.* at 19,373.

[39] *Id.*

[40] *Id.* at 19,374 (citing United States v. Zenith Radio Corp., 562 F.2d 1209, 1316 (C.C P.A. 1977), *aff'd*, 437 U.S. 443 (1978)).

Judicial Decisions on Department of Commerce 1984 Statutory Interpretation That CVD Law Does Not Apply to NME Countries

U.S. Court of International Trade Decision: *Continental Steel Corp. v. United States* (1985)

In *Continental Steel Corp. v. United States,* the U.S. Court of International Trade reviewed DOC's negative final subsidy determinations in the Czechoslovakian and Polish wire rod investigations and disagreed with the agency's conclusion that subsidies cannot by definition exist within a nonmarket economy.[41] As a result, the CIT reversed and remanded the case back to DOC for further investigation.

The CIT took specific issue with two of DOC's holdings. First, the CIT noted that DOC committed a "fundamental error" in its premise that a subsidy can only exist in a market economy.[42] Second, the CIT found that DOC's determination was "at odds with the plain meaning and purpose of the law," "contradicts judicial interpretations of the law," and is "inconsistent with past administration of the law."[43] Regarding its second point, the CIT noted that Section 303 of the Tariff Act of 1930 "makes no distinctions based on the form of any country's economy," and "on its face shows a meticulous inclusiveness and an unwavering intention to cover all possible variations of the acts sought to be counterbalanced."[44] According to the CIT, DOC's adoption of a *per se* rule that subsidies cannot exist in nonmarket economies served to effectively amend CVD law by administrative fiat and, therefore, was irrational, arbitrary, and contrary to law.[45]

Regarding DOC's determination that subsidies are purely a market phenomena and thus not applicable to nonmarket economies, the CIT found that the problem is essentially one of measurement and not one of meaning.[46] The CIT pointed to the application of antidumping law to nonmarket economies and noted that the use of surrogate or other substitute values for free market values does not deter DOC from determining dumping margins; therefore, the absence of free market values similarly should not serve to deter or prevent DOC from being able to calculate subsidy margins.[47]

U.S. Court of Appeals for the Federal Circuit Decision: *Georgetown Steel v. United States* (1986)

Subsequently, in *Georgetown Steel Corp. v. United States,*[48] the U.S. Court of Appeals for the Federal Circuit (CAFC) reversed the CIT and reinstated DOC's conclusions. The court, focusing first on DOC's holding that the terms "bounty and "grant" as contained in Section 303 of the

---

[41] Continental Steel Corp. v. United States, 614 F. Supp. 548 (Ct. Int'l Trade 1985).

[42] *Id.* at 550.

[43] *Id.*

[44] *Id.* at 551.

[45] *Id.* at 552.

[46] *Id.* at 554.

[47] *Id.* at 555.

[48] *Georgetown Steel Corp. v. United States,* 801 F.2d 1308 (Fed. Cir. 1986).

Tariff Act of 1930 were not intended to apply to nonmarket economies, held that the question could not be answered by relying on the statute's plain language.[49] The court noted that when the statute was initially enacted in 1897, there were no nonmarket economies; therefore, Congress had no reason to have addressed the issue.[50] According to the court, the fact that in the six subsequent amendments to the CVD statute Congress made no attempt to address the issue of the statute's application to nonmarket economies "strongly suggests that Congress did not intend to change the scope or meaning of the provision that it had first enacted in the last century."[51]

The court then discussed the two most recent amendments to the CVD laws and observed Congress's belief, as evidenced by both the acts themselves and their legislative histories, that

> changes in the antidumping law were necessary to make that law more effective in dealing with exports from nonmarket economies, coupled with its silence about application of the countervailing duty law to such exports, strongly indicates that Congress did not believe that the latter law covered nonmarket economies.[52]

In other words, according to the court, Congress intended to deal with imports from nonmarket economies being sold at unreasonably low prices under antidumping law, not CVD law.[53]

In conclusion, the CAFC, relying on accepted principles of administrative law, afforded DOC substantial deference with respect to its decisions regarding the application of CVD law to nonmarket economies. Specifically, citing the Supreme Court's 1984 decision in *Chevron U.S.A., Inc. v. Natural Resources Defense Council, Inc.*, which instructs courts faced with a statute that does not expressly speak to the issue at hand, or is ambiguous on the matter, to defer to an agency's interpretation of the statute provided it is reasonable and permissible, held that DOC had broad discretion in determining the existence of a subsidy under U.S. CVD law,[54] and consequently that DOC's conclusion that subsidies cannot be found in nonmarket economies was reasonable, in accordance with the law, and not an abuse of discretion.[55]

Post-*Georgetown Steel* Determinations

As a result of the CAFC's decision in *Georgetown Steel*, there were no other countervailing duty investigations of allegedly subsidized imports from nonmarket economies until 1991. That year, DOC did have occasion to examine a petition alleging the subsidization of ceiling and oscillating fans imported from China.[56] Although China was considered a nonmarket economy, the petition was based on the theory that this particular industry was sufficiently market-oriented that DOC

---

[49] *Id.* at 1314.

[50] *Id.*

[51] *Id.* (citing S. Rep. No. 249, 96th Cong., 1st Sess. 43 (1979), *reprinted in* 1979 U.S.C.C.A.N., v. 2, at 381, 429 (1979)).

[52] *Id.* at 1317.

[53] *Id.* at 1318.

[54] *See id.* at 1318 (citing United States v. Zenith Radio Corp., 562 F.2d 1209, 1219 (Fed. Cir. 1977). *aff'd* 437 U.S. 443 (1978)).

[55] *Id.* at 1318 (citing Chevron U.S.A., Inc. v. Natural Resources Defense Council, Inc., 467 U.S. 837, 842-45 (1984); Melamine Chemicals, Inc. v. United States, 732 F.2d 924, 928 (Fed. Cir. 1984)).

[56] Final Negative Countervailing Duty Determinations: Oscillating and Ceiling Fans From the People's Republic of China, 57 *Federal Register* 24,018 (June 5, 1992).

---

could reliably use the economic data provided by the industry itself consistent with the standards utilized for CVD investigations in market economies.[57]

According to DOC, to determine whether an industry is sufficiently market-oriented, a three-part test is utilized. First, "there must be virtually no government involvement in setting prices or amounts to be produced."[58] Second, the industry "should be characterized by private or collective ownership. There may be state-owned enterprises in the industry, but substantial state ownership would weigh heavily against finding a market-oriented industry."[59] Finally, "[m]arket-determined prices must be paid for all significant inputs, whether material or non-material (e.g., labor and overhead), and for an all-but-insignificant proportion of all the inputs accounting for the total value of the merchandise under investigation."[60] DOC ultimately concluded that, while some of the inputs for the ceiling and oscillating fans were in fact obtained from market sources, there remained a significant portion of the inputs that were not and, therefore, the industry as a whole did not qualify as a market-oriented industry.[61] As a result of this determination, DOC held that CVD law did not apply to the Chinese ceiling and oscillating fan industry.[62]

Some commentators and scholars have objected to this so-called market-oriented industry approach because the test, especially the third prong, almost guarantees that no such industries will be found.[63] In addition, some critics have contended that DOC's determination that "significantly all" factor input prices must be market-driven is ambiguous and may lead to arbitrary results. Such arbitrary results, according to critics, arguably play a role in creating uncertainty for nonmarket economy producers with respect to U.S. trade remedy laws.[64] Furthermore, it appears possible to argue that under this approach, a nonmarket economy can enact substantial market-based reforms while remaining immunized from CVD investigations.[65]

Although DOC's determination in *Oscillating and Ceiling Fans From the People's Republic of China* appeared to have opened the door to the potential application of CVD law to nonmarket economies, DOC did not accept another CVD petition against a nonmarket economy until 2006.

---

[57] *Id.* at 24,018.

[58] *Id.*

[59] *Id.*

[60] *Id.*

[61] *Id.* (stating that "[b]ased on our verification of the responses submitted in this proceeding, we determine that the fans industry in the PRC does not meet the third of these criteria").

[62] *Id.* at 24,019 (concluding that "we have determined that the PRC fans industry is not [a market-oriented industry]. As a result, we determine that the CVD law cannot be applied to the PRC fan industry.").

[63] Lawrence J. Bogard & Linda C. Menghetti, *The Treatment of Non-Market Economies Under U.S. Antidumping and Countervailing Duty Law A Petitioner's Perspective*, PLI Corp. Law and Practice Course Handbook, Series No. 789, 6-7 (1992); *see also* James K. Kearney & Jim Wang, *The Department of Commerce's Market-Oriented Industry Methodology for Nonmarket Economies in Antidumping Investigations The Responding Party's Perspective*, PLI Corp. Law & Practice Handbook Series No. 789, 255, 266-67 (1992).

[64] *See* James K. Kearney & Jim Wang, *The Department of Commerce's Market-Oriented Industry Methodology for Nonmarket Economies in Antidumping Investigations The Responding Party's Perspective*, PLI Corp. Law & Practice Handbook Series No. 789, 255, 266-67 (1992).

[65] *See* Lawrence J. Bogard & Linda C. Menghetti, *The Treatment of Non-Market Economies Under U.S. Antidumping and Countervailing Duty Law A Petitioner's Perspective*, PLI Corp. Law and Practice Course Handbook, Series No. 789, 9-11 (1992).

Application of CVD Law to Imports from China: *Coated Free Sheet Paper* and Beyond

On November 27, 2006, DOC announced that it had initiated a CVD investigation against China with respect to coated free-sheet paper.[66] Following an affirmative preliminary injury determination by the U.S. International Trade Commission,[67] DOC announced, via a notice published in the *Federal Register* on April 9, 2007, that it had made an affirmative preliminary subsidy determination in the CVD investigation with respect to these imports. DOC calculated preliminary estimated net countervailable subsidy rates ranging from 10.9% to 20.35%.[68]

Between the initiation of the investigation and DOC's preliminary findings, the government of the People's Republic of China sought an injunction from the U.S. Court of International Trade to prevent DOC from conducting the CVD investigation.[69] China argued that the court had proper jurisdiction to hear the claim for an injunction and that DOC was prohibited by *Georgetown Steel* from conducting CVD investigations.[70] Therefore, according to the government of China, Congress was required to pass a statute expressly authorizing the application of CVD law against nonmarket economies.[71] The United States responded by asserting that the court did not have appropriate jurisdiction to hear the claim until DOC issued its final determination in the CVD investigation; therefore, this case was not ripe for adjudication.[72] Further, the United States argued that there was no statutory or other legal prohibition on the application of CVD law to nonmarket economies; therefore, China's request for an injunction should be denied.[73]

The Court of International Trade declined to issue the injunction. Focusing primarily on the jurisdictional issues, the court held that the government of China and the other plaintiffs would have a "sufficient opportunity" to seek judicial review of their claims after DOC completed its investigation and issued a final determination.[74] While the court did address the applicability of *Georgetown Steel*—concluding that "it is not clear that Commerce is prohibited from applying countervailing duty law to [nonmarket economies]. Nothing in the language of the countervailing

---

[66] Notice of Initiation of Countervailing Duty Investigations: Coated Free Sheet Paper From the People's Republic of China, Indonesia and the Republic of Korea, 71 *Federal Register* 68,546 (November 27, 2006).

[67] Coated Free Sheet Paper from China, Indonesia, and Korea, 71 *Federal Register* 78464 (December 29, 2006).

[68] *See* Coated Free Sheet Paper From the People's Republic of China: Amended Preliminary Affirmative Countervailing Duty Determination, 72 *Federal Register* 17,484 (April 9, 2007).

[69] *See* Government of the People's Republic of China v. United States, 483 F. Supp. 2d 1274 (Ct. Int'l Trade 2007).

[70] *Id.* at 1277 (arguing that "[28 U.S.C. §] 1581(i) is available to them because the other potential vehicle for judicial review of their claims—filing suit under 28 U.S.C. § 1581(c) after Commerce completes the investigation—is manifestly inadequate.")(internal citations omitted).

[71] *Id.* at 1278 (asserting that "Commerce does not have the discretion to apply countervailing duty law to NMEs because the CAFC 'definitively ruled' that the countervailing duty statute 'may not be applied to imports from NME countries.'").

[72] *Id.* at 1279 (arguing that "it is not possible to separate the merits of the decision from those relating to jurisdiction ... because in order for this Court to determine whether this investigation is *ultra vires*, it would have to determine whether CVD law *could* be applied to an NME...."; further arguing that court lacked jurisdiction on ripeness grounds because final agency action had not yet been taken)(internal citations and quotation marks omitted).

[73] *Id.* at 1279-80 (asserting that "neither the countervailing duty statute nor Commerce's rules limit the agency's power to initiate countervailing duty investigations of NMEs. ... *Georgetown Steel* did not hold that the CVD law could never apply to NMEs under any circumstances, but only that Commerce's decision not to apply it in that case was reasonable.").

[74] *See id.* at 1281.

---

duty statute excludes [nonmarket economies]"[75]—its holding with respect to *Georgetown Steel* and its meaning is arguably *dicta*, as it does not appear to have been necessary to the conclusion that the court lacked jurisdiction.

In publishing its preliminary findings, DOC also issued a memorandum that directly confronted the *Georgetown Steel* precedent.[76] The memorandum provides a justification as to why China's economy in 2005, the period with which the investigation was concerned, and the so-called "Soviet-style economies" are distinguishable, such that it is now possible to apply CVD law to some nonmarket economy countries.[77]

It is important to note that the memorandum and preliminary CVD determination did not in any way change or alter China's formal status as a nonmarket economy.[78] Rather, the memorandum and justification focused on whether the rationale used to prevent CVD law from applying to nonmarket economies in 1984 remained true for modern-day China. The memorandum concerned itself with five major areas of the Chinese economy: wages and prices, access to foreign currency, personal property rights and private entrepreneurship, foreign trading rights, and allocation of financial resources.[79] While the specific economic analysis and details are beyond the scope of this report, the memorandum concluded that, unlike the so-called "Soviet-style economies" at issue in *Georgetown Steel*, China's present economy does not contain the same obstacles to determining the existence of subsidies. According to the memorandum,

> private industry now dominates many sectors of the Chinese economy, and entrepreneurship is flourishing. Foreign trading rights have been given to over 200,000 firms. Many business entities in present-day China are generally free to direct most aspects of their operations, and to respond to (albeit limited) market forces. The role of central planners is vastly smaller.... Given these developments, we believe that it is possible to determine whether the PRC Government has bestowed a benefit upon a Chinese producer (i.e., the subsidy can be identified and measured) and whether any such benefit is specific. Because we are capable of applying the necessary criteria in the CVD law, the Department's policy that gave rise to the *Georgetown Steel* litigation does not prevent us from concluding that the PRC Government has bestowed a countervailable subsidy upon a Chinese producer.[80]

---

[75] *See id.* at 1272 (court stated that "[a]lthough Plaintiffs allege that '[t]he CAFC has definitively ruled that the CVD law was not intended to be applied against NMEs' ... the *Georgetown Steel* court did not go so far as Plaintiffs claim and find that the countervailing duty law is not applicable to NMEs.... Rather, the *Georgetown Steel* court only affirmed Commerce's decision not to apply countervailing duty law to the NMEs in question in that particular case and recognized the continuing 'broad discretion' of the agency to determine whether to apply countervailing duty law to NMEs.").

[76] *See* Countervailing Duty Investigation of Coated Free Sheet Paper from the People's Republic of China - Whether the Analytical Elements of the *Georgetown Steel* Opinion are Applicable to China's Present-Day Economy, Memorandum from Shauna Lee-Alaia & Lawrence Norton, Office of Policy, Import Administration, to David M. Spooner, Assistant Secretary for Import Administration, March 29, 2007, *available at*, http://ia.ita.doc.gov/download/prc-cfsp/CFS%20China.Georgetown%20applicability.pdf (hereinafter *Georgetown Steel* Memo).

[77] *See id.*

[78] *See id.* at 2-4 (noting that DOC's recent review of China's nonmarket economy status concluded that "while China has enacted significant and sustained economic reforms, the PRC Government has preserved a significant role for the state in the economy. Indeed, the limits the PRC Government has placed on the role of market forces are sufficient to preclude China's designation as a market economy under the U.S. antidumping law.").

[79] *See generally, id.*

[80] *Id.* at 10.

Because the U.S. International Trade Commission made a negative final determination on injury,[81] CVDs were not imposed on the investigated merchandise.[82] Other CVD petitions were successful, however, resulting in the imposition of CVDs on NME country goods, beginning with a CVD order on Chinese carbon quality steel pipe in July 2008.[83] Twenty-four such CVD orders, covering goods from China and Vietnam, are now in place.[84]

Simultaneous Imposition of AD and CVD Orders on Same Nonmarket Economy Merchandise: Possible "Double Counting" of Subsidization

In most cases involving NME goods, petitioners have sought both antidumping and countervailing duty orders on the imports in question and thus most CVD orders are accompanied by an AD order on the same merchandise.[85] As discussed earlier, the treatment of China and Vietnam as nonmarket economy (NME) countries for purposes of antidumping investigations triggers a provision of U.S. law permitting DOC to use a "surrogate country" methodology to determine the fair market or "normal" value of products imported from the NME country. Assuming that an NME product is subsidized and the domestic sales price reflects the subsidy, the "surrogate country" methodology generally produces a higher normal value for the item than would result if the actual sale price in the NME country were used.

In determining an export or constructed export price of an item in any antidumping investigation—the price to which normal value is compared to determine the dumping margin— DOC is required under Section 772(c) and (d) of the Tariff Act of 1930[86] to make certain adjustments to the price, including increasing it by "the amount of any countervailing duty imposed on the subject merchandise ... to offset an *export* subsidy."[87] Neither this provision, which was added to the Tariff Act of 1930 in the Trade Agreement Act of 1979,[88] nor other provisions of antidumping law, expressly provide for an upward adjustment for CVDs imposed as the result of a domestic subsidy, that is, a government subsidy that is not tied to exportation but that may nonetheless benefit exported merchandise. The Commerce Department described the difference in treatment between the two as follows, referencing Article VI:5 of the General Agreement on Tariffs and Trade (GATT), which states that an imported product may not be "subject to both anti-dumping and countervailing duties to compensate for the same situation of dumping or export subsidization":

---

[81] Coated Free Sheet Paper from China, Indonesia, and Korea, 72 *Federal Register* 70892 (December 13, 2007).

[82] *See* Coated Free Sheet Paper from China, Indonesia and Korea, 72 *Federal Register* 70892 (December 13, 2007).

[83] Circular Welded Carbon Quality Steel Pipe from the People's Republic of China: Notice of Amended Final Affirmative Duty Determination and Notice of Countervailing Duty Order, 73 *Federal Register* 42545 (July 22, 2008).

[84] See U.S. Int'l Trade Comm'n, Antidumping and Countervailing Duty Orders in Place as of October 11, 2011, by Date of Order, at http://www.usitc.gov/trade_remedy/731_ad_701_cvd/investigations/active/index.htm (click on "AD/CVD Orders")[hereinafter, List of Current U.S. AD/CVD Orders]; Multilayered Wood Flooring From the People's Republic of China: Countervailing Duty Order, 76 *Federal Register* 76693 (December 8, 2011).

[85] *See id.*

[86] 19 U.S.C. §1677a(c),(d)(2006).

[87] 19 U.S.C. §1677a(c)(1)(C)(2006)(emphasis added).

[88] Trade Agreements Act of 1979, P.L. 96-39, §101, adding Tariff Act of 1930, Title VII, §772, 19 U.S.C. §1677a.

Domestic subsidies presumably lower the price of the subject merchandise both in the home and the U.S. markets, and therefore have no effect on the measurement of any dumping that might also occur. Export subsidies, by contrast, benefit only exported merchandise. Accordingly, an export subsidy brings about a lower U.S. price, which could be ascribed to either dumping or export subsidization, as well as the potential for double remedies. Imposing both an export-subsidy CVD and an AD duty, calculated with no adjustment for that CVD, would impose a double remedy specifically prohibited by Article VI ¶5 of the GATT. Thus, the only reasonable explanation for Congress' decision to provide for the … [addition to] U.S. prices of export-subsidy CVDs is protection against double remedies.[89]

The Commerce Department later expanded on the statutory distinction in this way:

The treatment of CVDs that arise out of domestic subsidies contrasts with the statutory treatment of CVDs that relate to export subsidies. The reason for the difference in treatment is that export subsidies are assumed to increase dumping margins by lowering the export price, but not the domestic price in the exporting country. Consequently, collecting both a CVD on an export subsidy and also the increase in the dumping margin resulting from that subsidy would constitute a double remedy for the export subsidy. Adding the CVD to the initial U.S. price lowers the margin by the amount the subsidy is presumed to have increased it, thereby preventing a double-remedy. On the other hand, domestic subsidies are assumed not to affect dumping margins, because they lower prices in both the U.S. market and the domestic market of the exporting country equally. As a result, there is no need for an adjustment to prevent a double remedy. Thus, in the most general germs, the statute stands for the proposition that dumping margins should not be calculated so as to double-collect CVDs.[90]

While the situation described may hold true with regard to AD investigations involving goods of market economy countries, it may not necessarily do so in AD investigations involving NME products where the surrogate country methodology is used to establish normal value of the merchandise in question and where a CVD order is imposed to remedy a domestic subsidy on the same merchandise. The U.S. Court of International Trade explained the distinction in *GPX Int'l Tire Corp. v. United States*, the 2009 decision involving CVDs on Chinese imports discussed later in this report:

Here, the export price is not being compared with the price of the good in the PRC in which case both sides of the comparison would be equally affected, but rather, export price, however it is affected by the subsidy, is compared with the presumptively subsidy-free constructed normal value. Without some type of adjustment for this, the imposition of AD duties could very well result in a double remedy.[91]

---

[89] Certain Cold-Rolled and Corrosion-Resistant Carbon Steel Flat Products From Korea: Final Results of Antidumping Duty Administrative Reviews, 62 *Federal Register* 18,404, 18,422 (April 15, 1997). Regarding the issue of GATT-consistency, see Trade Agreements Act of 1979, Statement of Administrative Action, H.Doc. 96-153, Part II, at 412, *as reprinted in* 1979 U.S.C.C.A.N., v. 2, at 683.

[90] Notice of Final Results of Antidumping Duty Administrative Review: Low Enriched Uranium From France, 69 *Federal Register* 46,501, 46,506 (August 3, 2004).

[91] GPX Int'l Tire Corp. v. United States, 645 F.Supp 2d 1231, 1242 (Ct. Int'l Trade 2009). The court referenced a report of the U.S. Government Accountability Office, which observed that "when the [constructed] normal value is compared with the export price, the difference will, at least in theory, reflect the price advantages that the exporting company has obtained from both export and domestic subsidies." *Id., quoting* U.S. Gov't Accountability Office, GAO-05-474, *U.S.-China Trade Commerce Faces Practical and Legal Challenges in Applying Countervailing Duties* 28 (June 2005), at http://www.gao.gov/products/GAO-05-474.

As explained in more detail below, the issue of double counting (or double remedies) arose not only in the court decision referenced above, but also in China's successful WTO challenge of several U.S. CVD orders on Chinese products, each case posing limitations on the ability of DOC to impose CVDs on NME imports.

World Trade Organization (WTO) Issues

WTO-Consistency of Imposing Antidumping and Countervailing Duties on Goods from NME Countries

The imposition of antidumping and countervailing duties by WTO Members on the products of NME countries implicates a variety of WTO agreements: the General Agreement on Tariffs and Trade 1994 (GATT 1994), particularly GATT Article VI; the Agreement on Antidumping; the Agreement on Subsidies and Countervailing Measures (SCM Agreement); and the WTO Accession Protocols of NME countries, such as China and Vietnam.

General Agreement on Tariffs and Trade 1994

Article VI of the GATT 1994 governs the imposition of AD and CV duties by WTO Members on the goods of all other WTO Member countries. It requires, inter alia, that any antidumping or countervailing duty imposed by a WTO Member on such products not exceed, respectively, the "margin of dumping"[92] or the amount of subsidization.[93] For purposes of Article VI, the dumping margin is the price difference that is determined when normal value and export price are compared.[94] As noted earlier, GATT Article VI:5 provides that no product of a WTO Member may "be subject to both anti-dumping and countervailing duties to compensate for the same situation of dumping or export subsidization." Article VI also generally requires that material injury be found before either type of duty may be imposed.[95]

While the text of Article VI does not itself distinguish between the products of market and nonmarket economy countries, an interpretative note to Article VI recognizes that AD duties may be imposed on the products of countries with government-controlled economies and that surrogate country data may possibly be used in making price comparisons involving normal value in such cases. The note states that

> It is recognized that, in the case of imports from a country which has a complete or substantially complete monopoly of its trade and where all domestic prices are fixed by the State, special difficulties may exist in determining price comparability for the purposes of paragraph 1 [of Article VI] and in such cases importing contracting parties [i.e., WTO

---

[92] General Agreement on Tariffs and Trade 1994 (GATT 1994), art. VI:2. at http://www.wto.org/english/docs_e/legal_e/gatt47_e.pdf.

[93] GATT 1994, art.VI:3.

[94] GATT 1994, arts. VI:1, VI:2.

[95] GATT 1994, art. (Art. VI:6)

Members] may find it necessary to take into account the possibility that a strict comparison with domestic prices in such a country may not always be appropriate.[96]

As recently explained by the WTO Appellate Body, this provision "allows investigating authorities to disregard domestic prices and costs of such an NME in the determination of normal value and to resort to prices in a market economy third country."[97] The Appellate Body also remarked that the note "appears to describe a certain type of NME, where the State monopolizes trade and sets all domestic prices" and "would thus not on its face be applicable to lesser forms of NMEs that do not fulfil both conditions, that is, the complete or substantially complete monopoly of trade and the fixing of all prices by the State."[98]

GATT Article XVI addresses subsidization itself, placing a notification requirement on WTO Members and containing specific obligations on the use of export subsidies. It provides that Members should seek to avoid the use of subsidies on primary products, that is, "any product of farm, forest, or fishery, or any mineral" in its natural or minimally processed form,[99] but that, if a party grants an export subsidy on such a product, the subsidy must not be applied in a manner which results in the grantor "having more than an equitable share of world export trade in that product" (Art. XVI:3). Article XVI also prohibits Members from granting, directly or indirectly, "any form of subsidy on the export of any product other than a primary product which results in the sale of the product for export at a price lower than the comparable price charged for the like product to buyers in the domestic market" (Art. XVI:4). Article XVI does not address subsidization by the types of NMEs referred to in GATT Article VI interpretative note.

Agreement on Antidumping

The WTO Agreement on Antidumping governs the application of GATT Article VI in actions taken under national antidumping laws or regulation.[100] The Agreement provides that antidumping measures may be applied "only under the circumstances" provided for in Article VI and "conducted in accordance with the provisions" of the Antidumping Agreement.[101] With regard to dumping by nonmarket economy countries, Article 2.7 expressly states that Article 2 of the Agreement, which sets forth obligations regarding the determination of dumping by national authorities in antidumping investigations, "is without prejudice to" the GATT Article VI interpretative note discussed above.[102] As stated by the WTO Appellate Body, this provision "thus incorporates … [the note] into the *Anti-Dumping Agreement*."[103]

---

[96] GATT 1994, ad art. VI, para.1, subpara. 2.

[97] Appellate Body Report, *European Communities—Definitive Anti-Dumping Measures on Certain Iron or Steel Fasteners from China*, para. 285, WT/DS397/AB/R (July 15, 2011)[hereinafter EC Fasteners AB Report].

[98] *Id.* para. 285, n.460.

[99] See GATT 1994, ad art. XVI, sect. B, para. 2.

[100] WTO Agreement on Implementation of Article VI of the General Agreement on Tariffs and Trade 1994 (Antidumping Agreement), art. 1, at http://www.wto.org/english/docs_e/legal_e/19-adp.pdf.

[101] *Id.*

[102] *Id.* art. 2.7.

[103] EC Fasteners AB Report, *supra* note 97, para. 285.

Agreement on Subsidies and Countervailing Measures

The WTO Agreement on Subsidies and Countervailing Measures (SCM Agreement), which expands considerably on obligations in GATT Articles VI and XVI, sets out obligations, rights, and remedies regarding the government subsidization of goods and the imposition of countervailing duties on subsidized imports.[104] The Agreement defines a subsidy as "a financial contribution by a government or any public body" within the territory of a WTO Member, or any form of income or price support, that confers a benefit. A financial contribution may take the form of (1) a direct or potential direct transfer of funds such as a loan or loan guarantee; (2) the foregoing of revenue "otherwise due"; (3) government provision of goods of services other than general infrastructure or government purchase of goods; or (4) government payments to a funding mechanism, or entrustment or direction of a private body to carry out one of the functions described above.[105]

The Agreement prohibits export subsidies and subsidies that are contingent on the use of domestic over imported products.[106] While the Agreement does not prohibit domestic subsidies, it requires that such a subsidy be shown to be specific to an industry and to cause adverse effects to the interests of a WTO Member to be remediable.[107] These are referred to as "actionable" subsidies. WTO Members may respond in two ways to subsidies that meet the Agreement's definition: (1) a direct challenge of the subsidy in a WTO dispute settlement proceeding, and (2) the imposition of countervailing duties on subsidized goods as the result of a domestic trade remedy proceeding.[108]

While the SCM Agreement does not expressly address the imposition of countervailing duties on the goods of NME countries,[109] it does provide an avenue for using cross-border benchmarks in measuring the benefit from a governmental financial contribution, the second portion of the Agreement's subsidy definition, in CVD proceedings involving these countries. In measuring such a benefit, WTO Members generally refer to market-based rates and prices in the subsidizing country. At the same time, a market-based benchmark may not be available in an NME country and thus, in such cases, the United States has used benchmarks based on rates or prices from one or more foreign market economy countries to make its benefit determinations.[110]

---

[104] The Agreement Establishing the World Trade Organization (WTO Agreement) provides that in the event of a conflict between a provision of the GATT 1994 and a provision of the SCM Agreement (or any other multilateral WTO agreement on trade in goods), the provision of the SCM Agreement (or the other WTO agreements) "shall prevail to the extent of the conflict." Agreement Establishing the World Trade Organization (WTO Agreement), Annex 1A, General interpretative note to Annex 1A.

[105] Agreement on Subsidies and Countervailing Measures (SCM Agreement), art. 1, *at* http://www.wto.org/english/docs_e/legal_e/24-scm.pdf.

[106] SCM Agreement, art. 3.

[107] SCM Agreement, arts. 1.2, 2, 5. Prohibited subsidies are considered specific *per se*. *Id.* art. 2.3.

[108] The SCM Agreement allows WTO Members to invoke the two mechanisms at the same time, but "with regard to the effects of a particular subsidy in the domestic market of the importing Member," the Agreement provides that only one form of relief is available: either a countervailing duty or a countermeasure (e.g., a tariff surcharge) imposed in the event that a defending subsidizing Member does not comply with a WTO decision against it. SCM Agreement, art. 10, n.35.

[109] Note that SCM Agreement did recognize that NME countries may be WTO Members, generally requiring WTO Members "in the process of transformation from a centrally-planned into a market, free-enterprise economy" to phase out prohibited subsidies, or make them conform with Article 3, within seven years from the date the WTO Agreement entered into force (by January 1, 2002), SCM Agreement, art. 29.

[110] *See, e.g.*, Coated Free Sheet Paper from the People's Republic of China: Amended Preliminary Affirmative Countervailing Duty Determination, 72 *Federal Register* at 17487-89.

Article 14 of the SCM Agreement, which addresses how a WTO Member may calculate a subsidy in terms of the benefit to the recipient, provides that "*any method* used by the investigating authority to calculate the benefit to the recipient … shall be provided for in national legislation or implementing regulations of the Member concerned and its application to each particular case shall be transparent and adequately explained," provided that the method is consistent with Agreement guidelines applicable to specified types of subsidies.[111] These subsidies are (a) government provision of equity capital; (b) government loans; (c) government loan guarantees; and (d) government provision of goods and services or government purchase of goods. With regard to the fourth category, Article 14(d) provides that

> the provision of goods or services or purchase of goods by a government shall not be considered as conferring a benefit unless the provision is made for less than adequate remuneration, or the purchase is made for more than adequate remuneration. *The adequacy of remuneration shall be determined in relation to prevailing market conditions for the good or service in question in the country of provision or purchase (including price, quality, availability, marketability, transportation and other conditions of purchase or sale).*[112]

In January 2004, the WTO Appellate Body (AB) found in *United States—Final Countervailing Duty Determination with Respect to Certain Softwood Lumber from Canada (U.S.—Softwood Lumber IV)* that, under Article 14(d), "an investigating authority may use a benchmark other than private prices of the goods in question in the country of provision, when it has been established that those private prices are distorted, because of the predominant role of the government in the market as a provider of the same or similar goods."[113] The AB went on to establish a limitation on the use of such benchmarks, requiring that their use must "relate or refer to, or be connected with, the prevailing market conditions in that country, and must reflect price, quality, availability, marketability, transportation and other conditions of purchase or sale, as required by Article 14(d)."[114] Nevertheless, the AB expressly refused to suggest or rule upon specific alternative methods that might be available to countries, noting that such a review would be appropriate only on a case-by-case basis.[115]

More recently, the AB, citing its findings in *U.S.—Softwood Lumber IV,* found further scope in Article 14 for the use of cross-border benchmarks. In China's challenge to U.S. CVDs discussed later in this report, the AB upheld a 2010 WTO panel decision finding that the United States had acted consistently with Article 14(d) in two CVD investigations in rejecting in-country private prices in China for calculating the benefit conferred by the provision, by state-owned enterprises, of hot-rolled steel inputs to Chinese companies. The AB ruling, which was partially adverse to the United States, set the following parameters for using a cross-border benchmark under Article 14(d):

---

[111] SCM Agreement WTO Agreement on Subsidies and Countervailing Measures, Art. 14, *available at,* http://www.wto.org/english/docs_e/legal_e/24-scm.pdf (emphasis added).

[112] *Id.* art. 14(d).

[113] Appellate Body Report, *United States—Final Countervailing Duty Determination with Respect to Certain Softwood Lumber from Canada,* para. 103, WT/DS257/AB/R (January 19, 2004).

[114] *Id.*

[115] *Id.* para. 106 (stating that "[n]or are we required to determine the consistency with Article 14(d) of all the alternative methods mentioned by the participants and third participants; such assessment will depend on how any such method is applied in a particular case.").

In sum, we are of the view that an investigating authority may reject in-country private prices if it reaches the conclusion that these are too distorted due to the predominant participation of the government as a supplier in the market, thus rendering the comparison required under Article 14(d) of the *SCM Agreement* circular. It is, therefore, price distortion that would allow an investigating authority to reject in-country private prices, not the fact that the government is the predominant supplier *per se*. There may be cases, however, where the government's role as a provider of goods is so predominant that price distortion is likely and other evidence carries only limited weight. We emphasize, however, that price distortion must be established on a case-by-case basis and that an investigating authority cannot, based simply on a finding that the government is the predominant supplier of the relevant goods, refuse to consider evidence relating to factors other than government market share.[116]

The AB further upheld the panel finding validating DOC's decision in these particular CVD investigations, finding that, in the dispute before it, "given the evidence regarding the government's predominant role as the supplier of the goods, that is, the 96.1 per cent market share, and having considered evidence of other factors, the Panel properly concluded that the USDOC could, consistent with Article 14(d) of the SCM Agreement, determine that private prices were distorted and could not be used as benchmarks for assessing the adequacy of remuneration."[117]

In addition to its evaluation of Article 14(d), the AB also ruled on the use of cross-border benchmarks under Article 14(b) of the SCM Agreement, a guideline for WTO Members calculating the benefit of a government loan in a CVD investigation. Article 14(b) provides that

> a loan by a government shall not be considered as conferring a benefit, unless there is a difference between the amount that the firm receiving the loan pays on the government loan and the amount the firm would pay on a comparable commercial loan which the firm could actually obtain on the market. In this case the benefit shall be the difference between these two amounts.

Again considering USDOC determination in CVD investigations involving Chinese goods, the AB stated that

> [it saw] no inherent limitations in Article 14(b) that would prevent an investigating authority from using benchmark interest rates on loans denominated in currencies other than the currency of the investigated loan, or from using proxies instead of observed interest rates, in situations where the interest rates on loans in the currency of the investigated loans are distorted and thus cannot be used as benchmarks. … In the absence of an actual comparable commercial loan that is available on the market, an investigations authority should be allowed to use a proxy for what 'would' have been paid on a comparable commercial loan that 'could' have been obtained on the market.[118]

---

[116] Appellate Body Report, *United States—Definitive Anti-Dumping and Countervailing Duties on Certain Products from China*, para. 446, WT/DS379/AB/R (March 11, 2011)(italics in original)[hereinafter U.S. CVDs AB Report].

[117] *Id.* para. 456.

[118] *Id.* para. 487.

The AB also upheld the panel's determination that the United States had acted consistently in rejecting domestic interest rates in this case:

> We do not consider, therefore, that the USDOC or the Panel was required to determine whether factors such as the government's predominant role as a lender, government regulation of interest rates, evidence of undifferentiated interest rates, and government influence over ... [state-owned commercial bank]-lending decisions, each resulted in interest rates that were lower than they otherwise would have been. In our view, it was, as the Panel found, sufficient for the USDOC to establish that all of these factors taken together distorted the commercial lending market such that comparing the interest rates of the investigated loans with observed rates in the same market would not be meaningful for the purposes of Article 14(b).[119]

At the same time, the AB found that the panel had not adequately determined whether the actual proxy benchmark used by the United States was consistent with Article 14(b), but could not complete the analysis due to an insufficient factual record in the WTO case.[120]

WTO Accession Protocols

The WTO Accession Protocols of NME countries, such as China and Vietnam, contain provisions governing price comparisons by other WTO Members in antidumping and countervailing duty investigations that support the use of surrogate countries, factors of production, or other "substitute benchmarks" in proceedings involving the goods of these countries.[121] The Protocols govern the countries' accession to the WTO and are an integral part of the WTO Agreement. While the language of Article 14 of the SCM Agreement is relevant to any discussion of the application of trade remedy laws to nonmarket economies, the Accession Protocols provide further guidance as to use of alternate methodologies with respect to particular WTO Member countries.

Article 15 of the WTO Accession Protocol of China, which is currently classified by the United States and other countries as a nonmarket economy,[122] states as follows:

> (a) In determining price comparability under Article VI of the GATT 1994 and the Anti-dumping Agreement, the importing Member shall use either Chinese prices or costs for the industry under investigation or a methodology that is not based on a strict comparison with domestic prices or costs in China based on the following rules:

---

[119] *Id.* para. 508.

[120] *Id.* paras. 510-537.

[121] *See* Protocol on the Accession of the People's Republic of China, WT/L/432 (November 23, 2001), *available at*, http://www.wto.org. Note also, e.g., the WTO Accession Protocol of Vietnam, WT/L/662 (November 15, 2006), which, at para. 2, incorporates language on antidumping and subsidy methodologies from the report of the WTO Working Party on the Accession of Viet Nam which is in may respects similar that in China's Accession Protocol. See WT/ACC/VNM/48, paras. 255, 527 (October 27, 2006).

[122] According to U.S. law, decisions to change China's classification to a market economy must be made subject to the statutory requirements established by §771(18)(B) of the Tariff Act of 1930, as added by the Trade Agreements Act of 1979. *See* Trade Agreements Act of 1979, P.L. 96-39 §771, 93 Stat. 144 (1979) (codified as amended at 19 U.S.C. §1677(18)(B) (2006)).

(i) If the producers under investigation can clearly show that market economy conditions prevail in the industry producing the like product with regard to the manufacture, production and sale of that product, the importing WTO Member shall use Chinese prices or costs for the industry under investigation in determining price comparability;

(ii) The Importing Member may use a methodology that is not based on a strict comparison with domestic prices or costs in China if the producers under investigation cannot clearly show that market economy conditions prevail in the industry producing the like product with regard to manufacture, production and sale of that product.

(b) In proceedings under Parts II, III and V of the SCM Agreement [i.e., WTO subsidy disputes and domestic CVD proceedings], when addressing subsidies described in Articles 14(a), 14(b), 14(c), and 14(d), relevant provisions of the SCM Agreement shall apply; however, if there are special difficulties in that application, the importing WTO Member may then use methodologies for identifying and measuring the subsidy benefit which take into account the possibility that prevailing terms and conditions in China may not always be available as appropriate benchmarks. In applying such methodologies, where practicable, the importing WTO Member should adjust such prevailing terms and conditions before considering the use of terms and conditions prevailing outside China.

…

(d) Once China has established, under the national law of the importing WTO Member, that it is a market economy, the provisions of subparagraph (a) shall be terminated provided that the importing Member's national law contains market economy criteria as of the date of accession. In any event, the provisions of subparagraph (a)(ii) shall expire 15 years after the date of accession [i.e., December 11, 2016]. In addition, should China establish, pursuant to the national law of the importing WTO Member, that market economy conditions prevail in a particular industry or sector, the non-market economy provisions of subparagraph (a) shall no longer apply to that industry or sector.

This language recognizes the inherent difficulties in calculating a subsidy or dumping margin using values obtained from nonmarket economies.[123] Focusing on CVD proceedings, the language indicates that, provided the use of cross-border benchmarks in CVD proceedings can be adjusted to meet the prevailing economic terms and conditions, the use of such benchmarks is both acceptable by China and permissible under WTO obligations. Indeed, the WTO Appellate Body has stated that Section 15(b) "affords importing WTO Members investigating Chinese imports additional flexibility in the methodology used to identify and measure subsidy benefits"

---

[123] Regarding antidumping proceedings, *see, e.g.*, EC Fasteners AB Report, *supra* note 97, para. 285. The WTO Appellate Body has made clear, however, that Section 15(a) applies only to determinations of normal value: "We do not consider that the references in paragraph 15(a)(i) to producers having to show that 'market economy conditions prevail … with regard to the manufacture, production and sale' of a product means that paragraph 15(a) permits any derogations also with respect to the determination of export prices. … Section 15 of China's Accession Protocol does not authorize WTO members to treat China differently from other Members except for the determination of price comparability in respect of domestic prices and costs in China, which relates to the determination of normal value. We consider that, while Section 15 … establishes special rules regarding the domestic price aspect of price comparability, it does not contain an open-ended exception that allows WTO Members to treat China differently for other purposes under the Anti-Dumping Agreement and the GATT 1994, such as the determination of export price or individual versus country-wide margins." *Id.* paras. 288, 290 (emphasis in the original)(footnotes omitted). See also Panel Report, *United States—Anti-Dumping Measures on Certain Shrimp from Viet Nam*, paras. 7.246-7.251 (WT/DS404/R (July 11, 2011)(adopted September 2, 2011).

in the situation described in that section.[124] While the use of cross-border benchmarks would thus not be a violation of WTO obligations on their face, the application of such benchmarks to a specific industry or imported product may still be subject to challenge on an "as applied" basis. It should also be noted that China's challenge to the U.S. application of CVD law to Chinese products, discussed above (and below), did not address the application of Article 15(b) to the disputed U.S. benefit analysis, but instead, as intended by the parties, focused solely on U.S. compliance with the guidelines set out in Article 14 of the SCM Agreement.[125]

China's WTO Challenge: *United States—Anti-Dumping and Countervailing Duties on Certain Products from China* (DS379)

China requested consultations with the United States in September 2008 regarding U.S. law and practice in antidumping and countervailing duty investigations involving Chinese imports.[126] In its subsequent panel request in December of that year, China made both "as applied" and "as such" claims, that is, it argued that both the application of U.S. antidumping and CVD law in particular investigations and, where the issue of double remedies was concerned, that the law in itself violated WTO obligations.[127] A panel was established in January 2009. In its "as applied" claims, China cited inconsistencies with the GATT articles, the WTO Agreement on Subsidies and Countervailing Measures (SCM Agreement), the WTO Antidumping Agreement, and Article 15 of China's WTO Accession Protocol, which sets out methodologies that WTO Members may use in determining price comparability in establishing whether and the extent to which dumping and subsidies exist, in four antidumping and four CVD investigations involving Chinese goods. Among other claims, China alleged the following:

- that in connection with U.S. findings that the alleged provision of goods for less than adequate remuneration fulfilled the definition of a subsidy under the SCM Agreement, DOC erroneously determined that certain state-owned enterprises (SOEs) were public bodies for purposes of the definition, that DOC failed to find that the alleged benefits that trading companies had received from SOE-provided goods were passed on to the producers of the merchandise that was the subject of the CVD investigations, and, in an argument analogous to that used in challenges to the use of "zeroing" in antidumping cases, that DOC improperly included in

---

[124] See U.S. CVDs AB Report, *supra* note 116, para. 436, note 401.

[125] *Id.*

[126] Request for Consultations by China, *United States—Definitive Anti-Dumping and Countervailing Duties on Certain Products from China*, WT/DS379/1 (September 22, 2008).

[127] Request for the Establishment of a Panel by China, *United States—Definitive Anti-Dumping and Countervailing Duties on Certain Products from China*, WT/DS379/2 (December 12, 2008). "As such" challenges have broader implications than "as applied" claims, which focus on the application of a statute, regulation, or practice to an individual situation, rather than on the norm itself. As explained by the WTO Appellate Body:

> By definition, an "as such" claim challenges laws, regulations, or other instruments of a Member that have general and prospective application, asserting that a Member's conduct—not only in a particular instance that has occurred, but in future situations as well—will necessarily be inconsistent with that Member's WTO obligations. In essence, complaining parties bringing "as such" challenges seek to prevent Members *ex ante* from engaging in certain conduct. The implications of such challenges are obviously more far-reaching than "as applied" claims.

Appellate Body Report, United States—Sunset Review of Anti-Dumping Measures on Oil Country Tubular Goods from Argentina, para. 172, WT/DS268/AB/R (November 29, 2004).

subsidy benefit calculations only those transactions that produced a positive benefit, while excluding transactions that yielded no benefit;

- that the United States had failed to demonstrate that the alleged provision of land and land use rights for less than adequate remuneration was specific to an industry or group of industries;

- that in connection with finding that the government had provided loans on preferential terms, that the United States had erroneously determined that certain state-owned commercial banks were public bodies, and also failed to find specificity;

- that in each case where the United States chose a benchmark outside of China in order to determine the existence and amount of any subsidy benefit, an action permitted under Article 15 of China's Accession Protocol, the United States had improperly rejected the prevailing terms and conditions in China as the basis for making its determinations;

- that in using its nonmarket economy (NME) methodology for determining dumping and imposing antidumping duties simultaneously with a determination of subsidization and the imposition of CVDs on the same product, the United States levied CVDs in excess of the subsidy found to exist in violation of the SCM Agreement, that is, an impermissible "double remedy"; that the levied antidumping and countervailing duties were in excess of the "appropriate" amounts, as called for in Article 9.2 of the AD Agreement and Article 19.3 of the SCM Agreement; that the United States failed to make a "fair comparison" between export price and normal value in its antidumping determination as required under the WTO Antidumping Agreement; that the United States imposed antidumping duties in excess of the amount of dumping found to exist; and that the United States failed to grant China the most-favored-nation (MFN) treatment required under Article I of the GATT by not according it "the same unconditional entitlement to the avoidance of a double remedy for the same unfair trade practice that it accords to imports of like products from the territories of other WTO Members"; and

- that in conducting the antidumping and countervailing duty investigations in question, the United States made various procedural errors involving notification and transparency and used improperly made adverse inferences from available information without having requested information from interested parties regarding the factual issue involved.

China also argued that U.S. law is inconsistent "as such" with U.S. obligations under the WTO Antidumping and SCM Agreements because it does not provide DOC with authority to avoid imposing an impermissible "double remedy" on goods from China when it uses surrogate country values for determining costs of production of goods made in a country designated a NME. Because imports from WTO Members with market economies are not subject to this treatment, China also considered this situation to be a violation of the GATT Article I, the GATT most-favored-nation article.

Panel Report

In a report publicly circulated on October 22, 2010,[128] the WTO panel rejected most of China's claims, as follows:

- Regarding the WTO-consistency of DOC's determinations in cited investigations that there was a *financial contribution* for purposes of the SCM Agreement's definition of a subsidy, the panel found that China had not established that the United States violated the SCM Agreement in determining that state-owned enterprises and state-owned enterprises (SOEs) and state-owned commercial banks (SOCBs) were "public bodies," agreeing with the United States that the term "public body" means "any entity that is controlled by the government."[129] The panel also rejected China's claim that the United States had violated the Agreement in determining that certain trading companies were "entrusted" or "directed" by the government to provide goods and services to producers of the investigated products.

- Regarding DOC's determinations of *specificity*, the panel rejected China's claims that DOC had improperly determined that lending by SOCBs to the off-the-road (OTR) tire industry was *de jure* specific, but also found that the United States had not acted consistently with the SCM Agreement in determining that the government provision of land-use rights in one investigation was regionally specific.

- Regarding U.S. *benefit* determinations, the panel found that China had not established that DOC violated the SCM Agreement by failing to conduct a "pass through" analysis in the OTR investigation to determine whether any subsidy benefits received by trading companies selling rubber inputs were passed on to OTR tire producers who purchased those inputs; by failing to "offset" positive with "negative" benefit amounts in the same investigation; and by rejecting Chinese prices and interest rates as benchmarks in various investigations. At the same time, the panel determined that DOC had acted inconsistently with the SCM Agreement in the OTR investigation (1) by not ensuring that the methodology used to determine the benefit to tire producers from purchases of SOE-manufactured inputs from trading companies did not result in a benefit that exceeded that conferred by the government's provision of the inputs, and (2) by using average annual interest rates as benchmarks for one company's U.S. dollar-denominated loans from SOCBs.

- Regarding China's *double remedy* claims, the panel rejected China's "as such" challenge, and reviewing its "as applied" claim, found that, while the panel did not doubt that in general the simultaneous imposition of an antidumping order based on NME methodology and a CVD order on the same merchandise likely results in the same subsidization being offset twice, China did not establish that double remedies were inconsistent with the SCM Agreement, Article VI:3 of the GATT, which prohibits the imposition of CVDs in excess of the amount of subsidization, or the GATT MFN article.

---

[128] Panel Report, *United States—Definitive Anti-Dumping and Countervailing Duties on Certain Products from China,* WT/DS379/R (October 22, 2010).

[129] *Id.* para. 8.79.

- Regarding alleged *procedural violations*, the panel found that China had not established that the United States violated the SCM Agreement by not granting China and various Chinese producers extra time to respond to certain questionnaires in the CVD investigations, but that the United States did violate an obligation under the SCM Agreement in using "facts available," that is, facts not provided by China or its companies, in determining the amount of SOE-provided hot-rolled steel that investigated producers purchased from trading companies.

Appellate Body Report

In an appeal by China,[130] the WTO Appellate Body (AB), on March 11, 2011, reversed the panel on two especially significant issues: the interpretation of the term "public body" and the permissibility of "double remedies."[131] The AB reversed the panel's finding that the term "public body" means an entity controlled by the government and thus its consequent finding that the United States had not violated the SCM Agreement in finding that certain SOEs and SOCBs qualified as such. The AB also completed the analysis on this point and concluded that DOC's determinations in the four CVD investigations that SOE input suppliers were public bodies were inconsistent with the Agreement, on the ground that a public body "must be an entity that possesses, exercises or is vested with governmental authority" and not merely an entity that is owned or controlled by the government.[132] The AB also concluded, however, that China had not established that DOC's determination that the SOCBs in the OTR investigation constituted public bodies was improper.

The AB upheld panel findings on specificity appealed by China. The AB also upheld two of the appealed findings approving DOC's use of foreign benchmarks in determining the subsidy benefit. The AB reversed the panel's rejection of China's claim that the foreign benchmark actually used by DOC to calculate the benefit from RMB-denominated SOCB loans in three investigations was inconsistent with Article 14(b) of the SCM Agreement, a provision governing the calculation of loan benefits, but, at the same time, found that it could not complete the analysis of China's claim under this article. The AB's reversal was based on its finding that the panel had not made an "objective assessment" of the issue, as required under Article 11 of the WTO Dispute Settlement.

In reversing the panel on the issue of "double remedies," the AB found that offsetting the same subsidization twice by the simultaneous imposition of antidumping duties based on NME methodology and countervailing duties is inconsistent with Article 19.3 of the SCM Agreement, which requires that, when a CVD is imposed on a product, it be levied "in the appropriate amount in each case." The AB also reversed related panel findings and found that, in the four sets of challenged antidumping and CVD investigations, because the United States had imposed duties concurrently without having assessed whether "double remedies" arose, the United States acted inconsistently with Article 19.3. As result, the AB also found that the United States was in violation of two other provisions of the SCM Agreement: Article 10, which requires WTO Members, inter alia, to ensure that the imposition of CVDs is consistent with Article VI of the

---

[130] Notification of an Appeal by China, *United States—Definitive Anti-Dumping and Countervailing Duties on Certain Products from China*, WT/DS379/6 (December 6, 2010).

[131] Appellate Body Report, *United States—Definitive Anti-Dumping and Countervailing Duties on Certain Products from China*, WT/DS379/AB/R (March 11, 2011).

[132] *Id.* para. 317.

GATT, and Article 32.1, which prohibits WTO Members from imposing a "specific action" against the subsidy of another Member except in accordance with the GATT, as interpreted by the SCM Agreement.

Implementation of WTO Reports

The Appellate Body report and modified panel report were adopted by the WTO Dispute Settlement Body (DSB) at its March 25, 2011, meeting. The United States and other WTO Members expressed considerable concern over both the AB's approach to the term "public body"[133] and to the legal reasoning and implications of the AB's finding on double remedies. As described in the DSB minutes, the United States noted that no provision of the Antidumping Agreement or the SCM Agreement restricted a WTO Member's ability to apply antidumping duties based on NME methodology and countervailing duties concurrently.[134] The United States further maintained that Article 19.3 of the Agreement, on whose language the AB based its conclusion, was not concerned with the definition and calculation of CVDs and "still less" with the concurrent application of antidumping and countervailing duties, but rather with the imposition and collection of CVDs, with the phrase "appropriate amounts" referring "simply to the fact that the CVD on particular imports may vary, even though a CVD should be imposed in a non-discriminatory manner."[135] The United States further stated that the report gave Members "no certainty in determining what would constitute an 'appropriate' amount of a CVD in a given situation" and that it "appeared to impose the entire burden of proving that there was no 'double remedy' on the importing Member."[136]

The United States added that the Appellate Body "appeared to impose significant administrative burdens on Members' trade remedy administrators in the situation of concurrent application of CVDs and NMEs," since ["[i]f required, measuring the effect of a subsidy on the export price of a good and other components of the dumping margin may involve highly complex economic and econometric analysis," a measurement that may entail "significant" difficulties.[137] In the U.S. view, this situation "raised serious questions about whether Members would be able to address trade-distorting subsidies by NME Members."[138]

The United States stated at the following DSB meeting that it intended to comply with the decision and that it would need a reasonable period of time in which to do so.[139] In July 2011, the United States and China agreed on a compliance deadline of February 25, 2012, which they later

---

[133] Dispute Settlement Body, Minutes of Meeting, March 25, 2011, at 18-19 (United States), 21 (Mexico), 22-23 (Turkey), 23-24 (European Union), 25 (Canada), 25-26 (Australia), 26-29 (Japan), 29-30 (Argentina), WT/DSB/M/294 (June 9, 2011).

[134] *Id.* at 19.

[135] *Id.* at 20.

[136] *Id.*

[137] *Id.* at 21.

[138] *Id.*

[139] Dispute Settlement Body, Minutes of Meeting, April 21, 2011, at 9, WT/DSB/M/295 (June 30, 2011). For further discussion of WTO dispute settlement procedures at the compliance phase, as well as the rights and obligations of the parties to the dispute at this phase, see CRS Report RS20088, *Dispute Settlement in the World Trade Organization (WTO) An Overview*, by Jeanne J. Grimmett.

extended to April 25, 2012.[140] In its January 2012 status report to the DSB, the United States stated that the United States Trade Representative (USTR)

> made a written request to the Secretary of Commerce to issue determinations under Section 129(b) of the Uruguay Round Agreements Act that would render US Department of Commerce ("Commerce") determinations in four original antidumping investigations and four original countervailing duty determinations of products from China—circular welded pipe, light-walled rectangular pipe, certain new pneumatic off-the-road tires, and laminated woven sacks—not inconsistent with the recommendations and rulings of the DSB."[141]

The United States continued:

> Commerce has been actively working on this matter and has issued questionnaires to Chinese respondents and to the Government of China, seeking additional information related to the issues on which the DSB adopted recommendations and rulings. Respondents have requested and Commerce has granted additional time for the submission of responses to the questionnaires. Commerce is analyzing responses provided to date and awaiting further responses from Chinese respondents and the Government of China.[142]

As discussed in the next section of this report, the U.S. Court of Appeals for the Federal Circuit ruled in December 2011 in *GPX Int'l Tire Corp. v. United States* that CVDs could not be imposed on NME goods under the existing CVD statute. In a rapid response to this ruling, Congress enacted P.L. 112-99, signed on March 13, 2012, which authorizes DOC to impose CVDs on such merchandise effective November 20, 2006 (thus covering the investigations at issue in the WTO dispute), and establishes procedures for the department to address double counting as of the date of enactment. The United States made note of the new law in its April 2012 status report to the WTO Dispute Settlement Body, mentioning the potential role of the statute in resolving the impermissible double counting found by the Appellate Body:

> The new legislation makes clear that where countervailing duties are applied to exports from a nonmarket economy country at the same time that anti-dumping duties, calculated using a "surrogate value" methodology, are applied to the exports, and evidence is presented that this has resulted in an increase in the dumping margin, Commerce may reduce the

---

[140] Agreement under Article 21.3(b) of the DSU, *United States—Definitive Anti-Dumping and Countervailing Duties on Certain Products from China*, WT/DS379/11 (July 8, 2011); Modification of the Agreement under Article 21.3(b) of the DSU, *United States—Definitive Anti-Dumping and Countervailing Duties on Certain Products from China*, WT/DS379/13 (January 19, 2012).

[141] Status Report by the United States, *United States—Definitive Anti-Dumping and Countervailing Duties on Certain Products from China*, WT/DS379/12 (January 10, 2012) [hereinafter January 2012 WTO Status Report]. Section 129(b) of the Uruguay Round Agreements Act, 19 U.S.C. §3538(b)(2006), authorizes DOC to issue new WTO-compliant dumping and subsidy determinations in response to adverse WTO reports, if requested in writing by the USTR. DOC must issue the new determination or determinations within 180 days after receiving the USTR's written request. After a determination is issued and the USTR consults with DOC and congressional committees, the USTR may direct the Commerce Department to implement the determination, in whole or in part. Implemented Section 129 determinations are prospective; that is, they apply to unliquidated entries of the subject merchandise (i.e., entries for which final duties have not yet been assessed) that are entered on, or withdrawn from warehouse, for consumption on or after the date on which the USTR directs Commerce to implement the determination. 19 U.S.C. §3538(c)(1)(b)(2006). Section 129 determinations are subject to judicial review in the U.S. Court of International Trade. 19 U.S.C. §1516a(a)(2)(B)(vii)(2006). The court's decisions may be appealed to the U.S. Court of Appeals for the Federal Circuit, whose decisions are reviewable by the U.S. Supreme Court. For additional discussion of Section 129 determinations, *see* CRS Report RL32014, *WTO Dispute Settlement Status of U.S. Compliance in Pending Cases*, by Jeanne J. Grimmett.

[142] January 2012 WTO Status Report, *supra* note 141.

antidumping duty to avoid what has been referred to as a "double remedy." Commerce is currently working to implement this new law, including as part of US efforts to implement the recommendations and rulings of the DSB in connection with this dispute.[143]

Notwithstanding its compliance activity, the United States did not fully comply by the April 25 deadline in the case. On May 11, 2012, the United States entered into a procedural agreement with China aimed at facilitating any compliance panel proceeding that may be requested by China and, if the United States is found to be out of compliance as a result of these proceedings, any sanctions request that China may pursue at that time.[144] To date, China has not made such a panel request.

Recent U.S. Judicial Decisions: CVDs May Not Be Applied to NME Country Goods

U.S. Court of International Trade Decisions: *GPX Int'l Tire Corp. v. United States* (2009-2010)

As the WTO case was proceeding, the U.S. Court of International Trade (USCIT), in a case involving CVDs on Chinese off-the-road tires, ruled in August 2010 in *GPX Int'l Tire Corp. v. United States*, that the application of CVDs on these imports concurrently with antidumping duties calculated under the NME methodology without making adjustments to avoid double counting was unreasonable and inconsistent with U.S. law.[145] In an earlier ruling involving the same CVD order, the USCIT stated that "[if] there is a substantial potential for double counting, and it is too difficult for Commerce to determine whether, and to what degree double counting is occurring, Commerce should refrain from imposing CVDs on NME goods until it is prepared to address this problem through improved methodologies or new statutory tools."[146] The court instructed Commerce that it "has a choice," explaining as follows:

---

[143] Status Report by the United States, *United States—Definitive Anti-Dumping and Countervailing Duties on Certain Products from China*, WT/DS379/12/Add.3 (April 13, 2012). As discussed later in this report, in the *GPX* proceedings in the U.S. Court of International Trade, where statutory authority to impose CVDs on NME products had been assumed and the court instead faulted the Commerce Department for not remedying double counting, the department believed that it had three options for addressing this issue: not to apply CVDs; to apply a market economy methodology in the concurrent antidumping investigation; or to offset the CVD against the duty deposit rate for the NME ADs. *GPX II, infra* note 145, 715 F.Supp.2d at 1344. The court found the department's choice of the third option to be unreasonable and not in compliance with the U.S. antidumping statute. *Id.* at 1345-46. The court also deemed the department's list to be "exhaustive" and "a tacit admission that, at this time, it is too difficult for Commerce to determine, using improved methodologies and in the absence of new statutory tools, whether and to what degree double counting is occurring." *Id.* at 1346. With the new statutory authority in hand, the Commerce Department, in its response to this portion of the WTO decision, will seemingly demonstrate whether it is now able to make the determination that the Court of International Trade assumed was too difficult for the department to make earlier.

[144] Understanding between China and the United States Regarding Procedures under Articles 21 and 22 of the DSU, *United States—Definitive Anti-Dumping and Countervailing Duties on Certain Products from China*, WT/DS379/14 (May 16, 2012).

[145] GPX Int'l Tire Corp. v. United States, 715 F.Supp.2d 1337 (Ct. Int'l Trade 2010)[hereinafter *GPX II*]. The use of double remedies by DOC on goods from China has also been challenged in a second case, *Guang Ya Aluminum Industries Co., Ltd. v. United States*, No. 11-00197 (Ct. Int'l Trade filed June 20, 2011).

[146] GPX Int'l Tire Corp. v. United States, 645 F.Supp.2d 1231, 1243 (Ct. Int'l Trade 2009)[hereinafter *GPX I*].

> ... The unfair trade statutes ... give Commerce the discretion not to impose CVDs as long as it is using the NME AD methodology. Thus, Commerce reasonably can do all of its remedying though [sic] the NME statute, as it likely accounts for any competitive advantages the exporter received that are measurable. If Commerce now seeks to impose CVD remedies on the products of NME countries as well, Commerce must apply methodologies, including methodologies that will make it unlikely that double counting will occur.[147]

DOC considered in the remand that it had three options—not to apply the CVDs, to apply the market economy antidumping methodology to either the company involved or the PRC, or to offset the CVD against the duty deposit rate for the NME ADs—and chose the third option.[148] In its August 2010 ruling, the USCIT held that the offset was "unreasonable" because it would always result in the unaltered NME AD margin and thus render concurrent AD and CVD investigations unnecessary.[149] The court also found that, "[p]erhaps even more importantly," this practice was inconsistent with Section 772(c)-(d) of the Tariff Act of 1930, 19 U.S.C. 1677a(c)-(d), which lists the specific offsets in dumping margin calculations that are "permissible" and held that the offset "does not comply with the statute."[150] The court further stated that it found DOC's tripartite list to be "exhaustive" and as such "a tacit admission that, at this time, it is too difficult for Commerce to determine, using improved methodologies and in the absence of new statutory tools, whether and to what degree double counting is occurring."[151] The court remanded again, ordering DOC not to apply CVD law to the goods of the exporter that had challenged the duties on this basis as well as to the goods of a second company even though it had not raised the issue in the litigation.[152]

U.S. Court of Appeals for the Federal Circuit Decision: *GPX Int'l Tire Corp. v. United States* (December 2011)

The U.S. government and domestic industry defendants appealed the *GPX* decision to the U.S. Court of Appeals for the Federal Circuit (CAFC). On December 19, 2011, a three-judge panel of the CAFC affirmed the lower court ruling, but on the ground that Congress had legislatively ratified the earlier agency and judicial interpretations that CVD law did not apply to NMEs and that, as a result, the Commerce Department may no longer interpret the statute as providing such authority.[153] The ruling thus prohibits DOC from imposing CVDs on the imports in question even if it were able to reasonably resolve the double counting issue or if there is no concurrent antidumping order on the merchandise under investigation. As a result, the department must seek legislative authority to apply CVDs to NME countries if it believes that the law should be changed.[154] The decision does not affect the authority of the Commerce Department to impose antidumping duties on NME country goods.

---

[147] *Id.*

[148] *GPX II*, 715 F.Supp.2d at 1344.

[149] *Id.* at 1345-46.

[150] *Id.* at 1345.

[151] *Id.* at 1346.

[152] *Id.* at 1346-47.

[153] GPX Int'l Tire Corp. v. United States, 666 F.3d 732 (Fed.Cir. 2011), at http://www.cafc.uscourts.gov/images/storeis/opinions-orders/11-1107.pdf [hereinafter *GPX III*].

[154] *Id.* at 745.

The CAFC, which engages in *de novo* review where statutory interpretation is involved, noted that "if after applying the traditional tools of statutory construction, the statute is ambiguous, 'statutory interpretations articulated by Commerce during its adjudications are entitled to *Chevron* deference.'"[155] In this case, however, the court found the CIT's reasoning on double remedies "problematic both because the extent to which the statute may prohibit double remedies is unclear, and because Commerce has determined that it is far from clear that double counting has in fact occurred."[156] In terms of *Chevron*, the court concluded that Congress had effectively spoken to the issue at hand and thus only one statutory interpretation was now allowed.

The court disagreed with the Commerce Department's contention that the plain statutory language mandating that a countervailing duty be imposed if DOC and ITC make the requisite subsidy and injury findings "requires that it impose countervailing duties when it can identify a subsidy, even in an NME country."[157] The court found that the statute is not "clear on its face" and "does not explicitly require" that CVDs be imposed on NME country goods.[158] Instead, the court viewed the question as whether "government payments in an NME economy constitute 'countervailable subsidies' within the meaning of the statute."[159] The court noted that its decision in *Georgetown Steel* had involved Section 303 of the Tariff Act of 1930, and that, although Congress had replaced the term "bounty or grant" as used in Section 303 with the term "countervailable subsidy" in the Uruguay Round Agreements Act of 1994 (URAA), Congress intended that the latter term be interpreted in the same way as the former, thus making *Georgetown Steel* applicable to the case at hand.[160] Further, while the Commerce Department had argued that *Georgetown Steel* did not independently interpret the statute but had accorded *Chevron* deference to what the court viewed as an ambiguous statute, the CAFC found that, even if *Georgetown Steel* did rest on *Chevron*, "the problem is that … Congress thereafter ratified the prevailing interpretation by amendment and reenacting the countervailing duty statute in 1988 and 1994, thereby requiring that we construe the statute as barring countervailing duties in the NME context."[161]

Noting that the principle of legislative ratification comes into play when Congress reenacts or amends a statute with awareness of a particular agency or judicial interpretation involving the statute involved and thus adopts that interpretation, the court found support for the principle in a variety of Supreme Court opinions, particularly *FDA v. Brown & Williamson Tobacco Corp.*,[162] the 2000 decision holding that the Food and Drug Administration lacked statutory authority to regulate tobacco.[163] Regarding the countervailing duty law, the court found evidence of congressional awareness of the earlier DOC interpretation of CVD law and the subsequent CAFC decision in Georgetown Steel upholding the DOC interpretation in (1) 1984 congressional hearings and, as Congress enacted changes to trade law in the Trade and Tariff Act of 1984, Congress's rejection of legislation that would have affected trade remedies involving NME imports; (2) the passage of the Omnibus and Competitiveness Act of 1988, during which

---

[155] *Id.* at 737 (*citing* Magnolia Metallurgy, Inc. v. United States, 508 F.3d 1249, 1355 (Fed.Cir. 2007); Pesquera Mares Australes Ltda. v. United States, 266 F.3d 1372, 1379 (Fed.Cir. 2001)).

[156] *Id.* (footnote omitted).

[157] *Id.* at 737-38.

[158] *Id.* at 738.

[159] *Id.*

[160] *Id.* at 738-39.

[161] *Id.* at 739.

[162] FDA v. Brown & Williamson Tobacco Corp., 529 U.S. 120 (2000).

[163] *GPX III,* 666 F.3d at 740.

Congress omitted in conference a provision that would have expressly applied CVD law to NME imports in direct response to *Georgetown Steel*; and (3) the reenactment of CVD law in the URAA of 1994, in which Congress changed the term "bounty or grant" to "countervailable subsidy" but did not make any changes to the law that "substantively affected countervailing duty law as it applies to this case."[164]

The court rejected DOC arguments that (1) Commerce's past practice did not extend to all NMEs, only to those for which subsidies could not be identified; (2) Congress made clear that CVD law should apply to NME countries when it enacted an appropriation in 2000 for "defending United States antidumping and countervailing duty measures with respect to the products of the People's Republic of China," the court finding instead that Congress intended this result only if Commerce found that China was no longer an NME country or that it had a market-oriented industry; and (3) the history of 2010 House-passed legislation providing that currency undervaluation may confer a countervailable subsidy evidenced Congress's understanding that CVD laws would apply to China.[165] Regarding the 2010 legislation, which was not enacted into law, the court stated that "it is well established that statements made in connection with unenacted legislation generally shed little light on the proper interpretation of a prior statute" and that "[i]f anything, the rejection of this proposal weighs against Commerce's argument that Congress intended countervailing duty law to apply to China."[166]

Subsequent Legislative and Judicial Developments

The Administration did not change its policy of treating China and Vietnam as nonmarket economy countries as a result of the *GPX* decision and instead sought legislation authorizing the Commerce Department to impose CVDs on NME products with regard to existing CVD orders as well as pending and future CVD investigations.[167] Legislation to respond to the *GPX* decision was introduced on February 29, 2012, and was quickly enacted by both Houses. H.R. 4105 (Camp) passed the House on March 6 and the Senate on March 7. The legislation was signed by the

---

[164] *Id.* at 740-43.

[165] *Id.* at 744-45.

[166] *Id.* at 745.

[167] Secretary of Commerce Bryson and USTR Kirk wrote to the Senate Finance Committee and the House Ways and Means Committee in January 2012 that the Administration was continuing to review "all options" in the litigation, "including a request for a rehearing by the full appellate court," but that it also wished to pursue legislation amending the CVD statute. *See* Letter to Hon. Max Baucus, Chairman, Senate Committee on Finance, from John Bryson, Secretary of Commerce, and Ron Kirk, U.S. Trade Representative, at http://insidetrade.com/iwpfile.html?file= jan2012%2Fwto2012_0129.pdf; *USTR Kirk, Bryson Tell Key Lawmakers Overriding GPX Ruling of Utmost Urgency,'* Daily Report for Executives (BNA), January 25, 2012; *Kirk, Bryson Urge Congress to Fix GPX Decision in Parallel to Judicial Review,* INSIDE U.S. TRADE, January 20, 2012, at 1; *Congress urged to ease China tariff rules,* FIN.TIMES, January 19, 2012, at http://www.ft.com. The letter stated that without legislation "should the decision of the court become final, Commerce will be required to revoke all CVD orders and terminate all CVD proceedings involving nonmarket economy countries, including 24 existing CVD orders on imports from China and Vietnam, as well as five pending investigations and two recently filed petitions." According to the letter, the Administration was seeking legislation "clarifying that the CVD law can be applied to subsidized goods from non-market economies, that CVD proceedings Commerce has already initiated on products from non-market economies are to continue, and that CVD determinations Commerce has made with respect to such products are to remain in effect." The United States had noted the potential economic effect of the decision in its January 2012 request to the CAFC to the extend the deadline for petitioning for a rehearing, stating that the existing countervailing duty orders on products of NME goods "represent[] billions of dollars in imports and ... [have] an effect upon producers in over 30 states."[167] U.S. Motion, *infra* note 169, at 2.

President March 13, 2012, and designated P.L. 112-99. Important considerations in the proposal were not only its temporal scope, but also whether it needed to deal with double counting of subsidization, the issue that arose in China's WTO case and that was also the focus of the U.S. Court of International Trade in its *GPX* rulings. The new statute generally authorizes the application of CVDs to NME products; makes this authority effective as of November 20, 2006; and prospectively amends antidumping law to provide a mechanism for the department to address double counting in simultaneous AD and CVD investigations.

As discussed earlier, Section 701(a) of the Tariff Act of 1930, 19 U.S.C. Section 1671(a), directs that countervailing duties be imposed on imported merchandise if (1) DOC determines that the "government of a country" or "any public entity within the territory of a country" is subsidizing the imports into the United States and (2) the U.S. International Trade Commission determines that the subsidized imports cause material injury or threat to a domestic industry. The new law amends Section 701 to add a new subsection providing that merchandise imported, or sold for importation, into the United States from a nonmarket economy (NME) country is covered by Section 701(a). The statute does not require DOC to impose CVDs on NME merchandise, however, if it cannot identify and measure government subsidies in an NME country "because the economy of the country is essentially comprised of a single entity." These provisions apply to all CVD proceedings initiated by the Commerce Department on or after November 20, 2006; all resulting actions by U.S. Customs and Border Protection (CBP); and all civil actions, criminal proceedings and other federal court proceedings relating to the initiated CVD proceedings or resulting CBP actions.

The statute also creates authorities and requirements aimed at addressing the double counting of domestic subsidization that occurs when simultaneous antidumping and CVD orders are imposed on the same NME merchandise and subsidization is captured both by the CVD and the dumping margin based on the higher normal value determined by use of surrogate country methodology. The bill amends U.S. antidumping law, as codified at 19 U.S.C. Section 1677f-1, to direct the Commerce Department to reduce an antidumping duty imposed on NME merchandise calculated by using surrogate-based normal value if the department determines that (1) a countervailable domestic subsidy "has been provided" with respect to the merchandise at issue; (2) the subsidy "has been shown" to have reduced the average price of imports of that merchandise "during the relevant period"; and (3) DOC can "reasonably estimate" the extent to which the countervailable domestic subsidy, in combination with the use of surrogate country methodology to determine normal value, has increased the weighted average dumping margin for the merchandise.[168] The duty is to be reduced by the amount of increase in the dumping margin estimated by DOC. The bill also provides that the reduction in the antidumping duty may not exceed the portion of the CVD rate attributable to the countervailable subsidy that is provided with respect to the merchandise at issue and that meets the three above-stated conditions.

The double counting provision applies to (1) all CVD proceedings initiated on or after the date of enactment and (2) all Section 129 dumping determinations, that is, new DOC dumping determinations issued under Section 129 of the Uruguay Round Agreements Act, to comply with WTO decisions, issued on or after enactment. Application to Section 129 dumping determinations would be subject to Section 129(c), which provides that such any such determination applies to

---

[168] A summary of H.R. 4105 issued by the House Ways and Means Committee indicates that the foreign exporter would demonstrate that the requisite reduction in export prices had occurred. House Committee on Ways and Means, Summary of "A Bill to Apply the Countervailing Duty Provisions of the Tariff Act of 1930 to Nonmarket Economy Countries, and For Other Purposes, at http://waysandmeans.house.gov/UploadedFiles/FINAL_CVD_One_Pager.pdf.

unliquidated entries of goods, that is, entries for which final duties have not been assessed, that enter the United States, or are withdrawn from warehouse, on or after the date that USTR directs DOC to implement the determination.

Shortly after the *GPX* was introduced, the U.S. government, meeting a March 5, 2012, deadline imposed by the U.S. Court of Appeals for the Federal Circuit (CAFC), petitioned the CAFC for a rehearing of the case *en banc*, that is, a hearing by the full court.[169] While the government had focused on *Chevron*-related arguments in its filing,[170] the enactment of legislation modified the questions before the court, which, the day after the new law was signed, requested the *GPX* litigants to submit arguments on the effect of P.L. 112-99 on further proceedings in the case. The United States asked that the appellate decision be vacated, arguing that it was not final and had been superseded by the new law, and that the case be remanded to the U.S. Court of International Trade for further proceedings in light of the new statute.[171] Importers argued that the effective date for the new CVD authority was unconstitutionally retroactive and that the court should affirm its earlier decision.[172]

On May 9, 2012, the CAFC, while not vacating its decision as requested by the government, granted the petitions for a rehearing and remanded the *GPX* decision to the U.S. Court of International Trade to address constitutional issues stemming from the different effective dates in the new statute.[173] In response to the CAFC's earlier directive, appellee importers had contended that the new legislation was unconstitutional because, in the words of the court,

---

[169] GPX Int'l Tire Corp. v. United States, Corrected Petition for Rehearing en Banc of Defendant-Appellant, United States, No. 2011-1107, at 1 (filed March 5, 2012)[hereinafter U.S. Corrected Petition for Rehearing]. The United States had requested an extension of the original February 2, 2012, deadline for such a petition to April 2, 2012. Defendant-Appellant United States' Motion for an Extension of Time to File a Petition for Rehearing and for Expedited Consideration, GPX Int'l Tire Corp. v. United States, No. 2011-1107 (Fed. Cir. January 20, 2012)[hereinafter U.S. Motion]. On January 24, the court granted the United States a one-time extension of the deadline to March 5, 2012. Case Summary, U.S. Court of Appeals for the Federal Circuit, GPX Int'l Tire Corp. v. United States, No. 2011-1107, Motions and Other Entries, Entry 127, filed January 24, 2012.

[170] Federal appellate rules disfavor rehearings, and a petition to the CAFC must state counsel's belief that the court's decision is contrary to specific U.S. Supreme Court decisions or CAFC precedents, that the appeal "requires an answer to one or more" enumerated "precedent-setting questions of exceptional importance," or both. FED. R. APP. P. 35(a); FED. CIR. R. PRACTICE 35(b)(2), at http://www.cafc.uscourts.gov/images/stories/rules-of-practice/rules.pdf.

The U.S. petition stated that the decision was contrary to several Supreme Court decisions, including *Chevron U.S.A. v. Natural Resources Defense Council, Inc.*, and identified the following two key questions for the court:

 (1) Whether the Court must defer to the Department of Commerce's reasonable interpretation of the countervailing duty statute when a prior Panel found the relevant statutory term to be ambiguous.

 (2) Whether the Department of Commerce is "locked in" to its putative 1980s interpretation of an ambiguous statute, based upon a theory of congressional ratification, because Congress reenacted the statute without expressly abrogating that interpretation or affirming it as reasonable.

U.S. Corrected Petition for Rehearing, *supra* note 169, at 1.

[171] Defendant-Appellant United States' Letter Brief in Response to Court Order, GPX Int'l Tire Corp. v. United States, No. 2011-1107, -1108, -1109 (Fed. Cir. March 23, 2012).

[172] Response of Plaintiffs-Appellees GPX International Tire and Hebei Starbright to Court's Request for Letter-Brief on New Legislation, GPX Int'l Tire Corp. v. United States, No. 2011-1107, -1108, -1109 (Fed. Cir. March 23, 2012); Plaintiff-Appellee Tianjin United Tire & Rubber Int'l Co., Ltd's Response to Court's Request for Letter-Brief, GPX Int'l Tire Corp. v. United States, No. 2011-1107, -1108, -1109 (Fed. Cir. March 23, 2012).

[173] GPX Int'l Tire Corp,. v. United States, No. 2011-1107 (Fed. Cir. May 9, 2012)(order granting rehearing and remanding to lower court), at http://www.cafc.uscourts.gov/images/stories/opinions-orders/11-1107-1108-1109%20order.pdf. The court also ruled that, prior to the new enactment, the CVD statute "did not impose a restriction (continued...)

(1) it attempts to prescribe a rule of decision for this case after our decision in *GPX* was rendered; and (2) it improperly creates a special rule applicable only to this case (or perhaps a few others) due to the different effective dates in the two provisions; it thus recreates a situation in which both antidumping and countervailing duties may be imposed, without providing a mechanism to account for potential double counting.[174]

The court dispensed with the separation-of-powers question raised by first argument, ruling that, because the *GPX* litigation was still pending on appeal when the legislation was enacted and therefore the court had not yet issued its mandate, Congress was not attempting to undo the final judgment of an Article III court, a legislative action prohibited under *Plaut* v. *Spendthrift Farm, Inc.*, 514 U.S. 211 (1995).[175] The court treated the second issue differently, however, considering it "a question of first impression as to which we have received only cursory briefing" and agreeing with the government that "'[t]o the extent that appellees ... argue that the new law is unconstitutional, such an argument should be decided by the trial court in the first instance.'"[176] The court also ordered that its mandate would issue on May 16, 2012.

Author Contact Information

Jeanne J. Grimmett
Legislative Attorney
jgrimmett@crs.loc.gov, 7-5046

Acknowledgments

This report is an updated version of a report originally prepared by Todd B. Tatelman, a former legislative attorney with the American Law Division, CRS.

(...continued)

on Commerce's imposition of countervailing duties on goods imported by NME countries to account for double counting," *id.* at 6, and thus the USCIT was wrong in finding that the imposition of both CVDs and antidumping duties on NME products under earlier law "amounted to 'unreasonable' double counting." *Id.* at n.3.

[174] *Id.* at 6-7.

[175] *Id.* at 7.

[176] *Id.* at 7-8.